A SAFARI
OF
AFRICAN COOKING

by

BILL ODARTY
(Bli Odaatey)

ILLUSTRATED BY SHIRLEY WOODSON

bp

BROADSIDE PRESS
Detroit, Michigan

Dedicated to my wife, Janet, and our lovely twins, Akweley and Akwetey; to Kojo, our handsome son, and Attah, our beautiful one who is not yet born; and to the people of the world who love to eat from Mother Africa's cooking pot.

ACKNOWLEDGMENTS

We sincerely thank the Embassies below for making it possible for us to produce *A Safari of African Cooking*:

Embassy of the Republic of Chad
Embassy of Burkina Faso
Embassy of the Empire of Ethiopia
Embassy of the Republic of Ghana
Embassy of the Republic of Ivory Coast
Embassy of the Republic of Kenya
Embassy of the Kingdom of Lesotho
    and the Permanent Mission of the Kingdom of Lesotho
    to the United Nations
Embassy of the Republic of Liberia
Embassy of the Malagasy Republic
Embassy of the Republic of Mali
Embassy of the Kingdom of Morocco
Embassy of the Republic of Nigeria
Embassy of the Republic of Senegal
Embassy of Sierra Leone
Embassy of the Somali Republic
Embassy of the Republic of the Sudan
Embassy of the Republic of Tunisia
Embassy of Zaire
Embassy of the Republic of Zambia

We also extend our special thanks to Commissariat General Au Tourisme et Au Thermalisme, Tunis, for letting us use the *Tunisian Gastronomy* as a reference in preparing *A Safari of African Cooking;* to the Mauritanian Mission to the United Nations and to the Ethiopian Tourist Organization, Addis Ababa, for allowing us to use their *Ethiopian-American Cook Book.*

Our sincere thanks to the Cultural Attaché of the Republic of Liberia who assisted us and gave us the *Open Door to Travel and Investment* book, published by the Department of Information and

5

Acknowledgments

Cultural Affairs, Monrovia, Liberia, 1967.

Many thanks to the Office of the Cultural Attaché of the Kingdom of Lesotho for their faithful cooperation with our venture, and to Mrs. Soukaina Fall, wife to the Senegalese Ambassador, who contributed to the Senegalese recipes.

We extend our warmest appreciation to Anita Bane who, with her past experience in African cooking, devoted her invaluable time to carefully review *A Safari of African Cooking*.

We give our thanks to Barbara Baita and Doris Burgess who gave us very rewarding advice; and to Mr. Rene G. Ralison, Charge d'Affaires, Embassy of Madagascar; and to Mr. J. R. Karanja, Commercial Attaché, Embassy of the Republic of Kenya.

Special thanks also go to Cathleen Laurie Hill and Linda C. Homburg who painstakingly typed the final copy of *A Safari of African Cooking*.

To Maureen Pflum and to many of our friends and staff at African-Odarty a note of thanks for their help and concern.

TABLE OF CONTENTS

Contents

Contents

PREFACE

The idea for this cookbook, *A Safari of African Cooking,* first originated at our African shop in Washington, D.C., when we were selling a West African cookbook, written by an American, which only partially covered any serious African cooking. One day I asked my wife to take the cookbook home and make the recipe for Ghanaian "Groundnut Soup and Rice." What she produced, by following the recipe, was closer to Spanish rice with chopped peanuts and was nothing like my home food. We were both so disappointed, and since I come from Ghana, my wife called the Ghanaian Embassy and asked if they had recipes for Ghanaian food. Indeed they did, and sent us several.

As the idea emerged, Maureen Pflum, a student from Georgetown University, assisted us as we began work on our *own* cookbook. We wrote to each African Embassy asking for recipes and wrote to some African countries, themselves, to research this project. We began to compile a collection of recipes which could be made with foods generally available in America, and also included recipe favorites that an African might expect to find in a cookbook of African food. In addition, Marie Adia Diop, a student of Georgetown University and a daughter of Mr. Alioune Diop, a Senegalese and publisher of *Presence Africaine* in Paris, helped us translate into English some recipes from French-speaking African countries. We took our recipes to wives of various African diplomats and African students who checked their country's section and tested the recipes.

Finally, we gave the nearly completed cookbook to Mrs. Anita Bane, an American who lived in Ghana for several years and had assisted in writing an international cookbook, published in Ghana. She made necessary changes she was confident would aid an American trying the recipes. We put all of these efforts together and came up with *A Safari of African Cooking.*

INTRODUCTION

We know that there are people who want to discover exciting African foods, but who may not have the opportunity to go to Africa to enjoy a safari, to hear the drumbeats, to see the jungles, and to eat the simple, but delicious, native food. This cookbook is for those people who would enjoy learning about, preparing, and eating African food.

If you wanted to entertain some friends or family with an unusual African dinner, where would you begin? First, you might think that you could borrow an African cookbook from an African acquaintance, then you might shop for the ingredients, and lastly, you would spend the rest of the day preparing the meal. If you have actually tried this, you know that preparing authentic African dishes is not as simple as it sounds. Your African friend won't have an authentic African cookbook that was published in Africa. She may take the time, however, to write down a few memorized recipes for you. But would you find CASSAVA or TEFF INJERA easy to prepare? Would you be able to translate directions like: "use one cigarette tin of rice" or "one shell of a small garden egg" into their American equivalents?

It was quite a challenge for us to adapt oral African recipes into everyday terms. In doing so, we ran into several problems. Each one of the recipes presented some type of problem. The primary characteristic of African recipes, like folk music, is that they are not written down. In fact, we found that very few contemporary Africans had any semblance of a written recipe to show us. In Africa, recipes are not needed in writing because every African girl learns how to cook by watching her mother from the time she can see the top of the huge family pot.

Another problem we found was that there is a wide difference in measuring food. Whereas most people are used to measurements in spoonfuls and cupfuls, an African will weigh foods by the gram or the ounce and use homemade measuring devices like a ladle or a fistful. We have made a chart for your convenience of these equivalents. As for measuring the number of servings, the majority of

African recipes originally would feed about 20 people. The African mother cooks for her entire family, including in-laws and friends. According to African custom, one is expected to invite to the meal any visitors at that time. Since most people are more formal about when and whom they invite to dinner, we have cut down the recipes for you.

You may find that many dishes come out looking a great deal like familiar ones, although the taste will differ considerably. This is understandable because the foods, being cooked from scratch, have a deeper, more natural flavor than frozen, packaged, or canned foods. The taste will vary greatly due to the type and amount of seasonings used. Out of necessity, the African people use a lot of spices where meat is scarce or not available, to give a variety of tastes to their starches. One spice in particular has an interesting story behind it. It is the red hot pepper (pilli-pilli). This particular spice, according to African belief, imparts a nutritive value, as well as making the blood circulate more quickly so that diseases have no chance to settle in the body. In addition, there is a saying that the more red pepper a mother uses in her cooking, the more she cares about her family's welfare.

Many cultures have influenced African cookery: black and white, yellow and tan. Styles of cooking range from Indonesian to Indian, from Arab to French cuisine, from pizza in Libya to wiener schnitzel in South Africa. Jews, Muslims, Christians and pagans will find African food compatible with their religious beliefs and a delight to their senses.

On browsing through this cookbook, you may wonder why we have included some recipes which require ingredients non-existent or difficult to obtain. We did this because we want this to be a fun, educational experience as well as a gastronomical one. We have included favorite dishes of a country even though some ingredients are hard to find, so that you may substitute or experiment for yourself. You will not find recipes from each of the forty-nine countries and territories, but since food is similar in related regions, we feel that all cuisines are covered.

We are sure your culinary talents will enjoy their journey to Africa. HAPPY HUNTING!

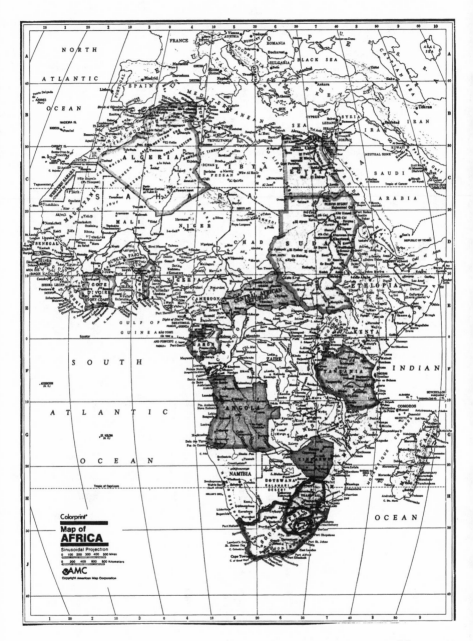

Map of
AFRICA
Sinusoidal Projection

Colorprint®

Copyright American Map Corporation

15

FACT SHEET
OF AFRICAN NATIONS

Name	Capital	Date of Independene	Former Sovereignty	Area 1000's of sq. mi.	Pop. Millions
Algeria	Algiers	7/3/62	15 Departments of French Republic	910	25.1
Angola	Luanda	11/11/75	Portuguese Overseas Province	481	9.0
Benin	Porto Novo	8/1/60	Autonomous Member, French Community	43	4.6
Botswana	Graborone	9/30/66	Bechuanaland, British protectorate	232	1.2
Burkina Faso	Ouagadougou	8/5/60	Autonomous Member, French Community	106	7.7
Rurundi	Bujumbura	7/1/62	Urundi, Part of Belgian UN Trust Territory of Ruanda - Urundi	11	5.2
Cameroon	Yaoundé	1/1/60	French UN Trust Territory of Cameroon and and Part of British UN Trust Territory of Cameroon known as Southern Cameroons	186	10.9
Cape Verde	Praia	7/5/75	Portuguese Overseas Province	2	0.34
Central African Republic	Bangui	8/13/60	Autonomous Member, French Community	241	3.0
Chad	N'Jamena	8/11/60	Autonomous Member, French Community	496	5.7
Comoro Islands	Moroni	7/6/75	French Overseas Territory	0.8	0.46
Congo Republic	Brazzaville	8/15/60	Autonomous Member, French Community	132	2.0
Djibouti	Djibouti	6/27/77	French Overseas Territory	9	0.33
Egypt	Cairo	6/18/53	British and the Farouks	387	55
Equatorial Guinea	Macabo	10/12/68	Spanish Overseas Province	11	0.4
Ethiopia	Addis Ababa	4/6/41 (Victory Day)	Italy, The Lion of Judah was dethroned in 1974 Last emperor: Haile Selassie 1	472	48
Gabon	Libreville	8/17/60	Autonomous Member, French Community	103	1.1

Name	Capital	Date of Independene	Former Sovereignty	Area 1000's of sq. mi.	Pop. Millions
Gambia	Banjui	2/18/65	British colony and protectorate	4	0.8
Ghana	Accra	3/6/57	British colony and protectorate and UN Trust Territory of British Togoland	92	14.0
Guinea	Conacry	10/2/58	Overseas Territory in French West Africa	95	6.0
Guinea-Bissau	Bissau	8/10/74	Portoguese Overseas Province	14	0.9
Ivory Coast	Abidjan	8/7/60	Autonomous Member, French Community	125	12.0
Kenya	Nairobi	12/12/63	British colony and protectorate	225	24.0
Lesotho	Maseru	10/4/66	Basutoland British colony	12	1.7
Liberia	Monrovia	1/8/47	Founded 1822 by USA for freed Black slaves who wanted to go back to the motherland (Africa)	38	2.5
Libya	Tripoli	12/24/51	Former Italian colony, jointly administered since WW II by France and the United Kingdom	680	4.3
Madagascar	Antananarivo	6/27/60	Autonomous Member, French Community	230	11.2
Malawi	Lilongwe	7/6/64	Nyasaland, British protectorate	46	8.1
Mali	Bamako	9/22/60	Soudanese Republic; independent from French Administration; Member of Federation of Mali	479	8.5
Mauritania	Nouakchott	11/28/60	Autonomous Member, French Community	398	1.8
Mauritius	Port Luis	3/12/68	British Colony	0.07	1.1
Morocco	Rabat	3/2/56	French and Spanish Protectorate; International Zone of Tanjier	172	25.4
Mozambique	Maputo	6/25/75	Portoguese Overseas Province	310	15.2
Namibia	Windhoek	3/21/90	Republic of South African mandate	321	1.2
Niger	Niamey	8/3/60	Autonomous Member, French Community	489	7.4

Name	Capital	Date of Independene	Former Sovereignty	Area 1000's of sq. mi.	Pop. Millions
Nigeria	Abuja	10/1/60	British colony, protectorate and part of British UN Trust Territory of Cameroons known as Northern Cameroons	357	115.2
Rwanda	Kigali	7/1/62	Ruanda, part of Belgian UN Trust Territory	10	7.3
Sao Tomé and Principe	Sao Tomé	7/12/75	Colony of Portugal	0.4	0.1
Senegal	Dakar	8/20/60	Independent from French Administration as Member of Federation of Mali	76	7.7
Seychelles	Victoria	6/29/76	occupied first by France, then Colony of Britain	0.2	0.07
Sierra Leone	Freetown	4/27/61	British colony and protectorate; Haven for freed black slaves 1787	28	4.3
Somalia	Mogadishu	7/1/60	Italian UN Trust Territory of Somalia and British Somaliland Protectorate	246	8.6
South Africa	Pretoria	1/9/10	British colony	472	35.6
Sudan	Khartoum	1/1/56	Anglo-Egyptian condominium	967	25.6
Swaziland	Mbabene	9/6/68	British protectorate	7	0.8
Tanzania	Dar Es Salaam	12/9/61	Tanganyika, British UN Trust Territory and and independent state of Zanzibar	365	24.8
Togo	Lomé	4/27/60	French UN Trust Territory	22	3.4
Tunisia	Tunis	3/20/56	French protectorate	63	7.9
Uganda	Kampala	10/9/62	British protectorate	93	16.8
Western Sahara	El Aiun	2/27/76	Spanish Overseas Province, annexed by Morocco and Mauritania	103	0.07
Zaire	Kinshasa	6/30/60	Belgian colony	906	34.0
Zambia	Lusaka	10/24/64	Northern Rhodesia, British protectorate	291	7.8
Zimbabwe	Harare	4/18/80	British colony: unilateral declaration of independence on 11/11/65	151	10.0

GLOSSARY

CASSAVA: a white root vegetable shaped like a sweet potato and containing a large amount of starch. When not available at your grocery, substitute sweet potato or yam.

COUSCOUS: a special type of wheat (semolina) grown in North Africa; fine, small-grained wheat.

COUSCOUSIERE: A special double boiler with holes in the top part like a colander. It is used specifically for steaming couscous. For a makeshift couscousiere, fit a colander tightly over a pot of the same size.

GARDEN EGG: an African name for a small eggplant.

MEALIE: the name for maize or corn in many African countries. Therefore, "mealie meal" substitutes for our "corn meal."

OKRA: a vegetable with sticky green pods, of the same type as squash or cucumber. Okra imparts a pale green color to a soup or sauce dish, as well as adding a delicious flavor.

PAPAYA: the fruit of the paw-paw tree, large and yellowish-orange in color. You might check at the supermarket for fresh papaya (or papaya nectar), or yellow melon may be substituted.

PLANTAIN: a large, starchy relative of the banana. Plantains are generally not so sweet as the banana, and are never eaten raw. The recipes will taste best if you can find plantains in your international supermarket, but otherwise substitute large, green, starchy bananas.

RISSOLES (turnovers): They are usually thin pastry filled with a seasoned mixture of minced meat or fish moistened with a white sauce and fried.

SEASONING: nearly all the African recipes we found do not call for a certain amount of salt and pepper, but just "seasoning to taste." You can make the recipes as "hot" as you want by adding red pepper instead of black. Use the following guide for determining the amount of salt needed:

1) in soups or sauces—1 tsp. to 1 qt. liquid
2) in batter or dough—1 tsp. to 4 cups flour
3) in cereals—1 tsp. to 2 cups liquid
4) in meats—1 tsp. to 1 lb. meat
5) in vegetables—1/2 tsp. when using 1 qt. of water

SHALLOT: a bulb vegetable a little smaller than an onion. Shallots perform the same function as onions in flavoring a dish.

SHORTENING: in North Africa, the basis for cooking is olive oil, while farther south, it varies from palm oil to peanut oil depending on the resources of the country. Your cooking will have a more authentically African flavor if you go to the trouble to use these oils. Do not use butter instead of oil; use butter only when it is called for specifically in a recipe.

STEWS: A stew in Africa often substitutes for a main dish. To increase the quantity of a stew, a white sauce may be added.

SUBSTITUTIONS: To avoid substitutions for spices and other ingredients, write VISAS CHOICE, INC. P.O. Box 539 Flushing, N.Y. 11368 or try local Spanish food markets.

TEMPERATURES: All temperatures in this cookbook are listed in Fahrenheit degrees unless otherwise noted.

FOREIGN EQUIVALENTS

MEASUREMENTS

African	American
1 gill	¼ cup
30 grams	1 ounce
454 grams	1 lb.
1 kilo	2.2 lbs.
1 liter	1.06 qts.
1 oz. butter	1 tbls.
1 ladle	¾ cup
1 oil tin	4.4 lbs.

COOKING TEMPERATURES

"Slow" oven	250-350 degrees F.
"Moderate" oven	350-400 degrees F.
"Quick," "hot" oven	400-450 degrees F.
"Very hot" oven	450-550 degrees F.

DEEP-FAT FRYING
TIMES AND TEMPERATURES

Cooked food	365-385 degrees F.	2-5 minutes
Uncooked batter or dough	350-365 degrees F.	2-3 minutes
Fish	350 degrees F.	5-10 minutes
Meat and poultry	385-390 degrees F.	5-8 minutes
Vegetables	385-390 degrees F.	4-6 minutes

FOOD WEIGHTS AND MEASURES

Baking Powder	1 oz. = 3 tbls.
Bananas	1 lb. = 3 medium bananas

Measurements

Beans (dried)	1 lb. = appx. 2 cups
(Lima)	1 lb. = 2-1/3 cups
(fresh)	1 lb. = 2 cups
Butter	1 lb. = 2 cups
Cloves (ground)	1 oz. = 4 tbls.
Coconut (shredded)	1 lb. = 5 cups
Corn meal	1 lb. = 3 cups
Cornstarch	1 lb. = 3 cups
Dates	1 lb. = 2 cups pitted
Eggs	1 lb. = 8-9 eggs
Eggs	1 cup = 5 whole eggs
Flour (white)	1 lb. = appx. 4 cups
(graham)	1 lb. = 3½ cups
Lard	1 lb. = 2 cups
Lemon juice	1 lemon = 4 tbls. juice
Oil	1 lb. = 2 cups
Peanuts (shelled)	1 lb. = 2-2/3 cups
Peas (in pod)	1 lb. = 2-3 servings
Pepper (whole)	1 oz. = 4 tbls.
(black)	1 oz. = 4½ tbls.
Rice	1 lb. = 2-1/3 cups uncooked
	1 cup raw = ¾ cups cooked
Salt	1 oz. = 1¾ tbls.
Spinach	1 lb. = 2½ qts. uncooked
Sugar (granulated)	1 lb. = appx. 2 cups
(brown)	1 lb. = 2½ to 2¾ cups

STANDARD WEIGHTS AND MEASURES

3 tsp.	1 tbls.
4 tbls.	¼ cup
5-1/3 tbls.	1/3 cup
8 tbls.	½ cup
16 tbls.	1 cup
16 oz.	1 lb.
1 fluid ounce	2 tbls.
16 fluid ounces	1 pint
1 cup	½ pint
2 cups	1 pint (1 lb.)
2 pints	1 quart (2 lbs.)
4 quarts	1 gallon
8 quarts	1 peck
4 pecks	1 bushel

CHAD

Chad, a country in the heart of Africa, is renowned for camels and livestock, and for traditional passways for caravans across the Sahara into central Africa. Camels are a major means of transportation in this country, since the rivers are impassible in the rainy season. Cotton is the most important crop in the south, followed by rice and peanuts.

Suggested Dinner Menu:

Squash with Peanuts, Okra and Meat Dish, Kague

KAGUE (Chadian Cakes)

The ingredients for these cookies from Chad are similar to our shortbread cookies, but rather than being baked in the oven, they are first allowed to rise and then browned in peanut oil.

1 tbls. fresh or powdered yeast
1 cup milk
2 tbls. peanut oil
1 cup sugar, granulated
4-5 eggs
4 cups white flour

Soften yeast in 1/4 cup warm water; set aside. Scald milk, add peanut oil and sugar. Stir and set aside to cool. Beat eggs into cooled milk mixture. Add two cups of flour to mixture and beat until light. Combine diluted yeast and beat again. Blend in remaining flour to make a moderately stiff dough. Knead about 5 minutes, until dough is smooth. Place in a greased bowl; cover and allow to rise in a warm place for about 1 hour. Do not allow dough to rise too much. Cut into small round pieces and fry in hot peanut oil until golden. Drain on paper towels. Sprinkle with granulated sugar and serve. Makes 8 dozen.

OKRA AND MEAT DISH

This meat and vegetable stew makes a well balanced meal when served with delicious boiled rice, yam or potatoes.

   2 lbs. beef or lamb, diced
   ¼ cup peanut or vegetable oil
   1 medium onion, chopped
   1 can (6 oz.) tomato paste
   8 medium fresh okra, sliced (or ½ package frozen okra)

Saute diced meat in peanut oil with chopped onion. Brown evenly. Add diluted tomato paste, sliced okra, and simmer until meat and vegetables are tender (1-1/2 hours). Add water as needed to make a sauce of suitable consistency if serving with boiled rice. Salt and pepper to taste. A variation of this recipe substitutes sweet potatoes for the okra. Serves 4.

SQUASH WITH PEANUTS

This tangy dessert can be served after lunch or dinner.

1 cup roasted peanuts, shelled
2 tbls. peanut oil
2-2½ cups cooked squash

Chop shelled roasted peanuts coarsely in a blender or meat grinder with a coarse blade. Add to squash with oil and salt to taste. Heat slowly for about 15 minutes and serve hot topped with white or brown sugar. Serves 4.

SWEET POTATO SALAD

4 large sweet potatoes
½ medium onion, chopped
lemon juice
peanut oil
2-3 medium potatoes

Boil sweet potatoes in their skins until tender (about 20-30 minutes. Cool, peel and slice. Add chopped onion, sprinkle liberally with lemon juice and oil; salt and pepper to taste. Garnish with tomato slices. Chill. Serves 6.

CONGO
Democratic Republic—
KINSHASA
(ZAIRE)

In this country, where Dr. Livingston died, palm oil is the basis of the one-meal-a-day diet; the national dish is Congo Chicken Moambe (p. 30), made generally with chicken cooked in palm oil and eaten with manioc leaves and rice. Large quantities of fish are consumed by the people living near the lakes, rivers, and sea. The local population also brews beer from bananas and alcohol from rice; large breweries for commercial beer are found in Leopoldville.

Suggested Menu Plan:

Dinner: Congo Chicken Moambe, Bread

CONGO: Baluba Tribe, Ceremonial Helmet mask with Beads, Shells, Cloth Decoration.

CONGO CHICKEN MOAMBE

Here are three methods to prepare the national dish of the Congo, Chicken Moambe. Methods I and III have similar sauces for the chicken, but the methods of cooking are different. Method II has a thicker sauce, as well as a different method for preparing the chicken.

Method I

  4-6 lbs. chicken
  ½ tsp. salt
  1 cup diced celery
  1 cup onion, minced
  6-oz. can tomato sauce

Cut up fresh (not frozen) chickens into pieces. Boil in enough salted water to cover until well done (1—1-1/2 hours). Take meat off bones and put back into salt water. Set aside. In another pan, fry celery and onion lightly for 3 minutes. Add this mixture and tomato sauce to chicken and let simmer for about 30 minutes. Serves 4-5.

Method II

    4-6 lbs. chicken
    ½ tsp. salt
    ½ tsp. red pepper
    1 cup onion, minced
    Dash of nutmeg
    ½ can tomato sauce (3 oz.)
    1 tbls. butter
    1 cup palm oil or peanut butter

Cut chicken up into pieces. Boil it in enough water to cover chicken, salt and pepper. Cook until well done (1—1-1/2 hours). In another pan, fry onion, nutmeg, tomato sauce and butter for about 3 minutes. Add chicken and cook in a covered pan for about 15 minutes. Add palm oil or peanut butter to thicken. Serves 4-5.

Method III

    4-6 lbs. chicken
    ¾ cup celery, diced
    1 tbls. onion, chopped
    ½ can (3 oz.) tomato sauce

Cut one frozen or fresh chicken into parts and brown on both sides in oil or shortening. Pour off oil and cook chicken in Dutch oven for 30-40 minutes. Fry celery and onion lightly for about 3 minutes. Add tomato sauce and cook 5 more minutes. Add this mixture to the chicken and let simmer for about 30 minutes. Serves 4-5.

GREEN PAPAYA JAM

If you would like a sweet surprise on your toast in the morning, we suggest you try green papaya jam. The papaya is a favorite fruit throughout Central Africa.

3 cups sugar
3 cups water
3 cups papayas, grated
½ tsp. vanilla
Juice of 1 lemon (4 tbls.)

Heat sugar and water for about 5 minutes until a syrup is formed. Add grated green papayas and cook slowly over low heat. When mixture thickens, remove from heat and add vanilla and lemon juice. Mix well. Pour into jars and seal. Fills two large jars.

GREEN PAPAYA PICKLES

½ cup sugar
1 cup water
1 dried hot pepper
½ cup vinegar
1 tsp. salt
1 stick cinnamon
1 large clove garlic, crushed
1 tbls. mixed pickling spices
2½ cups green papayas, diced

Papayas should be half-ripe. Make a syrup of the sugar, water, hot pepper, vinegar, salt, cinnamon and garlic. Put mixed pickling spices in a cheesecloth bag. Then boil this with the syrup 10-12 minutes. Add papaya and simmer 15 minutes until papaya is tender. Throw out the bag of mixed pickling spices and drain off the syrup from the papaya. Fill sterilized jars with the papaya, add a bit of the cinnamon stick to each jar, and fill up with the hot syrup. Seal. Makes 1-1/2 pints.

GREEN PAPAYA SOUP

We are sure you have never tasted anything like this before. After all, who would think of combining fruit and chicken bouillon? This soup should be about the consistency of thick pea soup.

    1 small onion, minced
    2 tbls. bacon fat or butter
    2 cups green papayas, diced
    2 cups boiling water
    2 chicken bouillon cubes
    1 tsp. salt
    ¼ tsp. hot red pepper
    1 tsp. cornstarch
    ¼ cup milk

Fry onion until transparent in fat. Add papaya, water, diluted bouillon cubes and seasoning. Simmer until papaya is mashable. Put through foodmill or strainer. Thicken with cornstarch dissolved in cold milk. Sauté tiny bread cubes in bacon fat for garnish. Serves 4.

ETHIOPIA

The variety of climatic conditions in Ethiopia produces a wide range of crops, including teff, which is used to make Injera (p. 41). Injeria is an unleavened bread that is a regularly eaten food. Tej, a honey-based dish, is usually made on special occasions. Coffee of high quality is grown in Kaffa, which is reputed to be the birthplace of the coffee plant. You will find that Ethiopian dishes come close to being the most time-consuming of all the African dishes, but the distinctiveness of the flavors will be well worth the extra time taken to prepare them.

Suggested Menu Plan:

Breakfast: Chechebsa and Coffee

Lunch: Lentil Wat and Hembasha

Dinner: Quanta, Chicken Stew, Teff Injera and Mint Tea

ETHIOPIA: Farmer with oxen.

CHECHEBSA (Ethiopian Pancakes)

1 ¼ cups "tef" or wheat flour
1 tsp. salt
¾ cup lukewarm water
1 cup butter, melted
1 tsp. cardamon
1 tsp. chili pepper

Sift flour and salt together into a large bowl. Add water, a little at a time, and knead well. Lightly grease a heavy skillet or griddle. Shape dough in pan to 1/2 inch thick pancake. Cook slowly on both sides until brown and crisp. Break into small pieces and put them in a bowl containing butter and remaining spices. Serve hot or cold. Serves 6.

CHICKEN WAT (Chicken Stew)

4-6 lbs. chicken, cut into pieces
1 ¼ cups red shallots or onions, chopped
3 cups water
¾ cup fresh red pepper
1 ¼ cup butter
1 ½ tsp. salt
1 tsp. ginger
1 tsp. black pepper

Clean the chicken and cut into serving-size pieces. Fry shallots or onions in oil until golden brown. Add a little water and red pepper; cook red pepper well, adding more water whenever necessary. After a few minutes, add butter and chicken. Cook until chicken is tender (about 1-1/2 hours). Add salt and ginger. Add the water and boil until about a quarter has evaporated. Remove from heat and sprinkle black pepper on the top of the "wat." Serve with hard-boiled eggs. Serves 4-6.

HEMBASHA (Wheat Bread)

1 tbls. dry yeast
5¼ cups lukewarm water
1½ cups white flour
7¼ cups whole wheat flour
2 tbls. salt
2 tsp, fenugreek
2 tsp. coriander
2 pods cardamon

Mix dry yeast with 1/2 cup warm water and let stand until bubbly. Mix white flour, 2-1/4 cups water and yeast mixture. Add wheat flour, 3 cups water and spices. Mix well. Keep the dough in a warm place and allow to rise until almost doubled in bulk. (Be sure that the bowl you have placed it in is big enough to accommodate the doubling.) Turn out onto a floured board and knead well. Divide into 6-8 pieces, and roll each piece into a round, flat loaf. Place on a greased baking sheet and prick with a fork. Bake in a hot oven (400-450 degrees) until light brown. Remove paper towels to cool, brush with warm water and cover with a cloth.

HYDROMEL "TEJ" (Honey Drink)

8¾ lbs, honey, raw with comb
17 qts. water
3-1/3 lbs. woody (gesho) hops

Mix honey with water and put into a wooden or glass container. Three days later, squeeze wax out of mixture. Cook gesho with some of the honey water: bring to a boil, simmer 15 minutes to avoid bitter taste, and put into container. Five days after adding hops, or when it is well-fermented, take hops out of container. Cover it well for 24 hours. The next day remove this "Tej" into another clean container which is well closed. Take out as much as required each time for use, and filter through a clean cloth before using. After 4-8 days it becomes strong and sediment collects. The "Tej" should be purified regularly.

LENTIL WAT (Lentil Stew)

1 ½ cups lentils
1 tbls. dried shallots or onions, finely chopped
3 tbls. red pepper (fresh)
¾ cup oil or shortening
2 tsp. garlic

Cook lentils in boiling water until tender (1-2 hours). Fry dried and chopped shallots or onions until brown. Add a little water and the red pepper; stir well. Add oil with a little more water, still cooking. Stir in cooked, mashed lentils. Be sure mixture does not stick on botom of pan. When a little more water has been added, salt to taste. Chop garlic finely, and add to pan. Allow to cook well, adding more water as necessary. Good when served cold as well as hot. Serves 4-6.

METIN SHURO (Spiced Vegetables)

This mixture of spiced vegetables is used in Metin Shuro Stew, a dish the Ethiopians take special pride in. Because of the preparation involved, we suggest you make this recipe in quantity; you will have requests to serve it again and again anyway.

2 ¼ cups peas
1 cup lentils
1 cup thick peas
1 cup beans
1 cup fresh red pepper
1/3 cup fresh ginger
1/3 cup garlic
½ cup red shallots or onions
1 ½ tsp. rue
1 ½ tsp. savory
3 tsp. fenugreek
2 tbls. sacred basil
3 pods cardamon

3 tsp. cloves
1 ½ tsp. cumin
1 ½ tsp. Bishop's weed
1 ½ tsp. cinnamon
1 ½ tsp. black cumin
1 ½ tsp. black Hildar Filfile
1 ½ tsp. coriander
½ cup salt
1 ½ tsp. "Kebebe Sine"

Wash peas, lentils, chick peas and beans; put them in boiling water for a few minutes. Drain off water. Roast each of the vegetables separately and dry in sunlight. When they are dry, grind separately into half pieces. Pick out black parts. Mix all vegetables together. Mix red pepper, ginger, garlic, red shallots (chopped), rue and savory, and dry outside in the sun. Roast fenugreek for a short period to remove raw taste. Mix vegetables with salt and add remaining spices. Grind this mixture into coarse spices. Grind whole mixture very finely and keep to use a little at a time. May be kept indefinitely in a good dry place.

METIN SHURO STEW (Spiced Vegetable Stew)

6 cups water
¾ cup oil or shortening
1 ½ cups "Metin Shuro" preparation*
Salt to taste

Boil water. Add oil, "Metin Shuro," and salt to taste. Cook well. Serve hot if added shortening is butter, but if oil is added, it tastes better cold.

───────

*See recipe for "Metin Shuro" preparation, p. 38.

MINCET ABESH (Beef Stew)

¾ cup red shallots or onions, chopped
¾ cup water
1/3 cup fresh red pedder
1½cups finely ground beef (or meat which has been
    chopped into very small pieces)
¾ cup butter
1 tsp. salt
1 tsp. "wat" spices*

Fry onions in oil until dark brown. Put in a little water and add red pepper. Stir, adding rest of water gradually until red pepper is cooked and milder in flavor. Add meat and cook for 1-1/2 hours or until tender. Add more water when necessary. Add butter, salt and "wat" spices. When meat is tender, serve hot. Serves 4-6.

*"Wat" spices

6 long peppers
3 tbls. black pepper
3 tbls. whole cloves
1 long nutmeg
pinch of tumeric

Roast spices over a low flame. Pound them in order to break up big pieces. Place a pinch of tumeric on the grinding stone and grind until a yellow coating of tumeric is spread over the working surface. Grind all the other spices together on the yellow grinding stone. These spices are added to the "wat" (stew) towards the end of cooking.

QUANTA (Dried Meat)

  2 lbs. beef or lamb
  2 tsp. salt
  ½ tsp. black pepper
  1 tsp. fresh red pepper

Trim fat from meat and soak up surface moisture with a cloth. Cut meat into long strips and rub with a mixture of the salt, pepper, and red pepper. Hang up strips in a clean cool place for 7-10 days to dry. Serve either raw for breakfast or roasted. Especially good as an hors d'oeuvre with cocktails. Serves 8.

TEFF INJERA (Unleavened bread)

  2-1/3 cups "teff" or wheat flour
  5-1/3 qts. water

Sift flour thoroughly. Mix water in gradually, rubbing out lumps with fingers. The mixture should be rather thick. Pour into bowl and leave uncovered for 2-3 days, or until fermented. (If there is batter saved from an earlier baking, add three cups to flour and water mixture and leave uncovered overnight.) Water will rise to the top of the mixture; discard this water.

Take out 1/2 cup of dough and add water to thin. Stir mixture continuously while cooking over in a medium heat, until it has become thick. Cool. Pour this mixture back into rest of dough and thin by adding cold water. Cover pan and let stand until mixture rises. Heat some fat or oil in a heavy griddle. To bake the "injera" fill a small pan with dough and pour it on heated skillet (medium heat) in a thin stream, starting from the outside and going in circles clockwise to the center. Cool slightly and then cover. Usually when the "injera" is cooked it will rise from the edge of the pan and can be easily removed to cool. Serves 5-6.

In Ethiopia, fresh "injera" is usually made every three days.

GHANA

Ghana is one of the richest tropical African countries. It is the world's leading producer of cocoa as well as a major mineral exporter shipping gold, diamonds, manganese and bauxite to world markets. The staple food of Ghana is cassava, which the family cook will boil, mash or mill to make "garri." When the Ghanian woman takes time out from household duties she may be found selling palm wine while her husband may be weaving "kente" cloth on a hand loom. "Kente" is woven with silk thread in strips six inches wide. The strips are sewn together to make the large toga-like robes both men and women wear on ceremonial occasions.

Suggested Menu Plan:

Breakfast: Kose or Krakro with Koko

Lunch: Garri Foto, Fruit in season

Dinner: Groundnut Soup, Komi, Kelewele

ABOLOO (Dumplings)

Aboloo is mainly prepared and eaten by the Ewe people of Ghana and Togo. It tastes delicious with fried (deep fat) fish and hot pepper. It tastes a little sour by itself.

3 cups corn meal
3½ cups water
2 tbls. wheat flour

GHANA: Young man weairng traditional robe of kente cloth.

43

½ tsp. baking powder
1 tsp. salt

Mix cornmeal with enough water to form dough. Divide dough into three parts. With one part, prepare a thick porridge with 3 cups boiling salted water. Pour cooked porridge into a mixing bowl and cool until warm. Mix in remaining two parts of uncooked dough. Combine flour with baking powder and salt; add to dough and beat thoroughly. Add about 1/2 cup more water to form a soft dough. Set in a warm place in a covered container to rise until top of dough splits open and looks porous. Cook by steaming in aboloo leaves (or aluminum foil may be substituted). Aboloo is finished cooking when it feels firm and spongy and has no starchy taste. Serves 8.

AKPLE (Cassava-Corndough Balls)

Akple is an Ewe specialty which is delicious when served with meat or fish as a main dish.

6 cups water
1 ½ lbs. fermented corndough
½ lb. cassava dough
1 tsp. salt

Bring water to a boil and add salt. Combine corn and cassava doughs thoroughly with a little cold water. Using a wooden spoon, pour mixture into boiling water and stir continuously to avoid lumping. Taste for salt. Continue stirring until the dough is well-cooked (it should look creamy and have no starchy taste). Form into little balls. If akple is too hard, add some hot water by lifting the porridge and letting the water run down the sides of pan to bottom. Allow to boil and stir until well mixed. Akple is ideal as an accompaniment to Okra Soup (p. 49) or Dodo (p. 58). Serves 6.

GARDEN EGG STEW (Eggplant Stew)

Garden Egg Stew is best served with Aboloo, Akple, Komi or Kenke.

2 medium (2 lb.) eggplants
1 cup oil or shortening (palm oil is best)
6 medium onions, sliced
4 oz. salt fish
3 medium tomatoes, sliced
1 tsp. ground red pepper
1 lb. smoked herring

Wash eggplant and boil until tender (10-15 minutes). Remove skins if desired. Heat oil and fry onions, salt fish, and tomatoes in that order. Stir to prevent sticking and add red pepper. Mash and add eggplant. Add smoked herring and the liquid left from boiling the eggplant, if desired. Simmer for 20 minutes. Serve hot. Serves 6.

GARRI FOTO (Garri Stew)

"Garri" is milled cassava. Although cassava is hard to get in the United States, it is not unavailable. This is a very popular dish in Ghana, and you can substitute rice for the garri in this recipe if you do not have the time to locate cassava in your local community.

1 lb. garri
1 cup water
4 medium onions, chopped
6 large tomatoes
4 eggs (or 1 tin of sardines or ½ tin of corned beef)
fresh ground ginger (optional)
1 oz. dried ground shrimp
fresh red pepper
½ cup oil or shortening

Sprinkle garri with cold salted water until the grains absorb all the water but are not saturated. Allow grains to swell. Wash and cut up onions and tomatoes. Make eggs into an omelette using some of the chopped onions. Fry the rest of the onions in hot oil until lightly browned; add tomatoes and salt and pepper to taste. (Add ground ginger at this point if desired.) If sardines or corned beef are used, fry with onions and tomatoes. When tomatoes are well-cooked, add ground shrimp and garri. Mix well making sure you scrape the bottom of the pan so lumps of garri don't form. Add half the omelette to this mixture, stirring over low heat. *Garri Foto* is served hot garnished with omelette and parsley, as a meal in itself, or as an accompaniment to rice, beans or stew. Serves 4.

GROUNDNUT SOUP (Peanut Soup)

With Ghana as an African exporter of peanuts, it is no wonder that they have combined peanuts with plentiful fowl in this delicious soup.

    4-6 lbs. chicken, cut into sections
    2 medium onions, chopped
    4 medium tomatoes
    1 lb. groundnut paste or 1¾ cups peanut butter
    2 fresh red peppers or ground red pepper to taste
    12 cups water

Brown chicken and onions in a large saucepan until golden. Salt to taste. Add just enough cold water to cover the chicken and add tomatoes. Bring to a boil; lower heat and simmer for 15 minutes. Remove tomatoes, scoop out pulp, and add pulp to stock. Mix the peanut butter into a smooth cream with hot stock from the saucepan. Pour this creamed paste into the saucepan and add water and pepper. Season to taste. Cook slowly until the oil rises to the top of the soup. If chicken becomes tender before oil rises, remove chicken to prevent it from disintegrating; return to pot when soup is cooked. Serves 6.

GROUNDNUT TOFFEE (Peanut Toffee)

    1¼ cups granulated sugar
    1 tbls. butter
    2 cups roasted peanuts

Melt sugar in a saucepan and brown lightly (5 minutes). Fold in butter. Fold in nuts until well-coated (5 minutes). Dampen a pastry board and pour the toffee onto it. While still hot, roll mouthful quantities into balls with a wooden spoon. Cool and store. Cover tightly to prevent stickiness.

KELEWELE (Plantain or Banana Appetizer)

This is a spicy, tangy food which can be served in many ways. It is superb served with chili, perfect as a breakfast meal, and fun for afternoon snacking.

3 lbs. (6 large) plantains or bananas
1 tsp. powdered ginger
½ tsp. salt
½ tsp. ground red pepper
2 tbls. water
3 cups oil or shortening

Wash and peel plantains or bananas and cut crosswise into 1/2 inch slices. Mix ginger, salt, and red pepper with water. Drop plantain slices into mixture and stir around with fingers, place in hot oil and deep-fat fry until golden brown. Serves 6.

KOMI or KENKE (Corndough Balls)

This is the main dish of all the coastal people of Ghana and especially those people who live in Accra, the capital. Komi has a very sharp taste and is often served with deep-fried fish or meat dishes.

2 lbs. fermented corndough
1 tsp. salt
2 cups water
corn shooks (husks) and stalks

Divide corndough into two portions. (See directions for making fermented corndough on page 43). Put water on to boil and add salt.

Put one portion of corndough into boiling water. Mix well with a wooden spoon to make *Aflatta* (boiled corndough). Add *Aflatta* to uncooked portion of corndough, and mix well into smooth, heavy paste with hands. Divide into four portions. Wrap each in clean wet corn shooks (or aluminum foil). Cover bottom of saucepan with strips of cornshooks and stalks. (Saucepan should be large enough so that the four balls of dough will form one layer only.) Cover with a heavy cloth or corn shooks and add a tight-fitting lid. Cook for two hours or until the komi is soft and light in color. Serve hot or cold. Serves 4.

KOSE (Bean Scoops)

    1 ½ cups beans
    4 tsp. water
    1 egg
    2 small onions
    1 small tomato
    2 cups cooking oil

Soak beans overnight and remove skins. Grind into paste and beat paste in a bowl to incorporate air. Add water and egg, beat again. Grind onions and tomatoes separately. Salt and pepper to taste and then add to paste. Deep-fry in hot oil in scoops until brown. Serve hot or cold. Serves 4.

KRAKRO (Fried Plantain or Banana and Corndough)

    ½ cup cornmeal
    2 lbs. (4 large) ripe banana or plantain
    1 tsp. salt
    ½ tsp. red pepper
    2 cups vegetable oil or shortening

Mix the cornmeal with enough water to make a thick pudding. Leave out to ferment for three days; scrape off the top portion because it is probably spoiled. Wash and peel bananas or plantains; cut up and mash until very soft. Mix with corndough, salt and pepper.

Let stand for 30 minutes. Scoop dough into balls and fry in hot oil until brown. Serve hot or cold with beans or chili. Serves 8.

OKRA SOUP

½ lb. meat
1 tsp. salt
3 medium onions, sliced
2 medium tomatoes, mashed
4 cups water
½ lb. crabmeat
2 medium eggplants
¼ lb. smoked shrimps, ground
½ lb. smoked fish, boned
1 lb. young tender okra, chopped
½ cup palm oil or vegetable oil

Wash and cut meat into several pieces. Add salt, sliced onions, mashed tomatoes, pepper to taste, 1/2 cup water; let simmer 10 minutes. Add crab and remaining water and cook meat until tender. Split eggplant and add to soup. Add ground shrimps, boned fish, chopped okra (very small pieces). Season to taste. Add oil. Let soup cook uncovered for about 10 minutes. Stir frequently to avoid over-boiling or burning the bottom of the pan. When soup is ready, remove from heat and leave uncovered for a minute or two before covering, to keep the slippery consistancy typical of *Okra Soup*. Serve hot with *Akple* (see p. 44). Serves 4.

SPINACH STEW

4 lbs. stewing beef
2 cups cooking oil or shortening
2 lbs. fresh spinach
2 lbs. fresh collard greens
6 medium onions, sliced
3 medium-sized fresh fish (porgies, rockfish or
    red snapper)—optional

small piece of codfish
4 medium tomatoes
3-4 eggs
1 cup water
2 tsp. red pepper cayenne

Wash and cut up stewing beef; sprinkle with a little salt and onion powder. In pan, add just enough water to cover and boil for 1-2 hours until tender. Slice tomatoes and onions; wash greens and boil until soft (10-20 minutes). Strain leaves and keep the liquid. Mash and grind seeds of tomatoes, and leaves. If fish is desired, clean and cut into reasonable pieces, season with a little onion salt and oil; bake in a slow oven for 20 minutes. Brown beef and fish in hot oil (including piece of cod fish) together with onions and tomatoes. Add mashed leaves, fried ingredients and a small quantity of the liquid from leaves. Lightly beat and add eggs. Add pepper and a pinch of salt to taste. Simmer slowly for about 45 minutes. Stir occasionally. Serve hot with boiled rice, boiled potatoes or spaghetti. Serves 8.

STUFFED EGGPLANT

1 large eggplant
1 small onion
2 tbls. salad oil
¼ cup breadcrumbs
2 tbls. grated Parmesan cheese
1 tsp. salt
1 tsp. oregano
dash of pepper
1 egg, slightly beaten

Cook whole eggplant in enough boiling salted water to cover until tender but still firm (about 30 minutes). Meanwhile, cook onion in oil until limp; set aside. Lift eggplant from water, and cut in half lengthwise when cool enough to handle. Scoop out the inside meat with a spoon leaving the shell intact. Add eggplant pulp to onion and mash mixture with fork. Stir in breadcrumbs, cheese, seasonings and egg. Pile mixture into eggplant halves and bake 30 minutes at 350 degrees. Delicious served with beef. Serves 6.

TUO ZAAFI (Flour Dumplings)

    1 ¼ cups whole millet flour
    9 cups water

Mix 2/3 cup flour with 2 cups water and let stand overnight. Divide the dough into two parts. To one part add the rest of the flour and stir until thickened. With the other part, prepare a thick porridge with 7 cups boiling salted water. Add first half and continue cooking, stirring until a smooth, sticky paste is formed. Test with fingers: they should come free. Serve hot or cold with soup.

TWISTED CAKES

    2 cups flour
    ½ cup butter
    1 cup sugar
    ½ tsp. grated nutmeg
    pinch of salt
    1 egg
    milk, enough for moistening (about 2 tbls.)
    1 cup oil or shortening

Cream butter and sugar. Mix nutmeg, salt and egg and fold well into butter and sugar. Add flour a little at a time and mix well. Add just enough milk to moisten the mixture so that it can be rolled out without crumbling. Roll the pastry into 1/4 inch thick sheet, and cut into 1/2 inch wide strips. Taking three strips at a time, place the strips and cut each plait into 1 inch pieces. (If you wish to make it easier, simply roll into balls). Heat oil to the boiling point, lower heat and fry the pieces of pastry until golden brown. Spread white paper towels on a flat surface, spoon out the fried pastry and let drain. Eat hot or cold. Serves 10.

IVORY COAST

Women in the Ivory Coast area use the plentiful Plantain or banana in their everyday cooking. The recipe for **Fried Plantain or Banana Fingers** (p. 55) is only one of the many ways to use plantains or bananas. The plantain or banana may also be stewed, baked, steamed, boiled, or roasted for soups, porridges, and even as liqueurs.

Suggested Dinner Menu:

Fried Plantain Fingers, Foutout with Lamb, Melon Fingers with Lime

IVORY COAST: Helmet Mask, Kornbla Society
Rhythm Pounder, Ge Tribe with superimposed female, male and bird forms.

FOUTOUT WITH LAMB

White corn meal, hominy grits, or cream of rice
4 green leaves (optional) or aluminum foil
2 lbs. lamb steak
3 tbls. peanut oil or other cooking oil
1 pkg. sliced, quick-frozen okra
¼ oz. pkg. dehydrated onion soup mix
1½ cups boiling water
4 tbls. canned tomato sauce
4 tbls. chunky peanut butter
½ tsp. chili powder

According to package directions for 4 servings, make up a stiff mush of white corn meal, hominy grits, or cream of rice. With buttered hands, shape the mush into balls and make a depression with your thumbs on both sides. Wrap this foutout in green leaves or aluminum foil, and keep warm in hot water, while you prepare the lamb.

Cut lamb steak into 1/2 inch cubes. Brown quickly in peanut oil for about 3 minutes. Remove lamb, and in the same skillet, lightly sauté the okra for 3 minutes. In a separate saucepan, stir the onion soup mix into boiling water. Cover and simmer for 10 minutes, stirring occasionally. Add tomato sauce and peanut butter; stir until smooth. Season with chili powder to taste; add more than a tablespoon if you like the authentic African "heat." Add sautéed lamb and okra to the sauce. Cook together 2 minutes longer. Serve with foutout. Serves 4.

FRIED PLANTAIN OR BANANA FINGERS

This is a delicately flavored accompaniment to meat or fish; or it can be served as a dessert when topped with sugar and cinnamon instead of pepper.

> 2 plantains or 4 bananas
> lemon juice
> peanut oil (about 1/3 cup)
> crushed corn flakes or breadcrumbs
> black pepper

Cut plantains or bananas into quarters lengthwise and then into halves crosswise, making eight fingers for each plantain or banana. Allow to stand 10 minutes covered with lemon juice. Roll in fine crumbs or crushed corn flakes and fry quickly in peanut oil 1/2 inch deep until crispy brown. Sprinkle to taste with black pepper. Serves 4.

MELON FINGERS WITH LIME

This is a most refreshing dessert or appetizer.

> 1 large chilled Honeydew or Persian melon
> 1 lime

Cut the melon into eighths or sections about 1 inch wide. Do not cut all the way through. On a large plate, spread out the sections like a flower. Remove all seeds, etc., and garnish with leaves if you wish. Place a cluster of lime sections in the center of the tropical flower. Serves 8.

KENYA

Kenya, the well-known hunting country, is situated astride the equator. The nation is chiefly agricultural and has increased its domestic production threefold since 1947. Corn, wheat, millet, cassava, sweet potatoes, barley, and sugar cane are Kenya's subsistence crops. Pig, sheep and cattle are raised also. Coffee is the largest export in this country, followed by sisal and tea.

Suggested Menu Plan:

Breakfast: Beans and Tea or Coffee

Lunch: Muhogo Tamu, Rice or Bread

Dinner: Esstata, Dodo, Sima and Spinach

DODO (Kenya Steak Supreme)

1 lb. rump steak
2 tbls. oil or shortening
¼ tsp. baking soda
1 ½ cups water
2 ripe tomatoes
½ cup peanut butter

Cut steak into 4 portions. Heat oil and quickly brown meat on both sides (a nice rich brown, but not burnt). Remove pan from flame and add 1 cup water, 1 tomato, peeled and chopped, soda, and salt to taste. (Kenyans use the crushed refined stone form omukhelekha.) Return to heat and simmer until liquid evaporates to 1/2 cup. Mix peanut butter with 1/2 cup water and add to meat. Continue simmering until meat is tender and sauce is of a coating consistency. To serve, arrange meat neatly in a meat dish and carefully coat with the sauce. Garnish with 1 tomato sliced or quartered. Serve with *Sima* (p. 60) and spinach. Serves 4.

ESSTATA (Plantain or Banana Appetizer)

10 plantains or bananas (big and ripened)
½ cup sour milk
3 eggs
½ cup butter
pinch of salt
1 lb. corn flour

Peel bananas or plantains and mix well with milk, eggs, butter, pinch of salt, using a wooden spoon or an eggbeater until well-blended. Add corn flour and mix into a soft dough. Pour into a greased bowl ("sufuria") and wrap in foil paper to seal. Stand the bowl or "sufuria" in a big pan containing hot water, or in a steamer, and cover the boiler or steamer tightly. Steam for 1-1/2 hours. Serve hot with stewed mushrooms, other vegetables, or stews. It is a bit sweet, but very appetizing. The leftovers can be cut into slices and fried in oil or reheated in the oven. Serves 20.

MUHOGO TAMU (Yam Stew)

1 large (2 lb.) cassava or yam (muhogo)
1 onion, chopped
1 lb. beef or mutton, diced
1 tomato, diced
¾ tsp. ground tumeric
3 green chili peppers, ground (pili-pili mbichi)
green coriander, ground
1 lemon
1 fresh coconut (nazi)—grated
1 tbls. oil or sohrtening

Cut muhogo into small pieces and boil in enough water to cover until cooked (about 20-30 minutes). Strain off water. Cut and fry onion in oil; when brown, add meat and tomato. Salt and pepper to taste. When meat is cooked (about 1-1/2 hours), add strained muhogo to it. Grate coconut meat. Add hot water and extract the milk from the grated coconut meat by squeezing with the hand or through a muslin cloth. Add this coconut milk to the meat and muhogo and return to heat. Add tumeric, ground peppers, and coriander. Cook for another 1/2 hour. This dish can be served with bread or boiled rice. Serves 4.

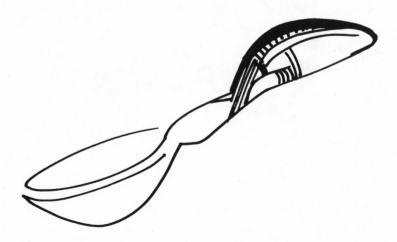

Kenya

SIMA (Grilled Cornflour Balls)

2 cups water
1½ cups cornflour
1 tbls. butter
1 egg
milk

Add flour little by little to boiling water, stirring with a wooden spoon. Continue cooking over low heat until a thick consistency is achieved. Add butter to make the consistency lighter. Cook 10 minutes, stirring until the outside of the dough forms a transparent film (this means that the starch is cooked). Mix egg with small amount of milk and dip spoonful-size balls of the dough into this mixture. Brown in oven or under broiler for 2-3 minutes. Serves 4.

TAMALE PIE

½ lb. ground meat (preferably some pork)
3 cloves garlic, minced
1 medium onion, chopped
2½ cups canned tomatoes or 6 oz. tomato sauce
1 tsp. salt
1 tsp. sugar
2 tbls. chili powder
pinch oregano
pinch marjoram
pinch cumin

1 cup water
1 cup corn meal
1½ tsp. salt

1 can whole kernel corn
½ cup sliced black olives
½ cup grated cheddar cheese
1 can pinto or kidney beans, already cooked

Blend the first group of ingredients into a sauce. (Omit the last three spices if prepared chili powder is used.) Cook corn meal in salted water, stirring until mush is thick. Line bottom and sides of 9 x 13 flat baking dish with this mush. Add half the sauce. Then spread on a layer of black olives, and a layer of cooked red beans. Pour rest of sauce over this and sprinkle with grated cheese. Bake at 350 degrees for about 40 minutes. The sauce may be frozen and keeps very well. Serves 6.

LESOTHO

Wool, mohair, and cattle are the chief exports of this south African country with a population of under one million. The staple crop of the region is mealie meal (ground-up corn). Like most Africans, they love meat, and will eat it whenever it is available. You will find that the recipes from this country are wonderful when you want quick and simple, but very tasty dishes.

Suggested Menu Plan:

Breakfast: Egg or Mixed Rissoles and Coffee
Lunch: Stuffed Cabbage and fruit
Dinner: Mealie Meal Salad, Meat Stew, Lesotho Scones

CURRIED EGGS

    8 eggs
    ¼ cup oil or shortening
    2 small onions, chopped
    2 tsp. curry powder
    ¼ cup flour
    1 cup milk

Boil eggs for 10 minutes. Leave in cold water to cool. Heat oil and fry onions until light brown. Add curry powder and flour; salt and pepper to taste. Boil for 1 minute. Stir in milk and cook slowly for about 10 minutes. Shell eggs and cut in half. Put them in a dish and pour the sauce over them. Serves 4.

LESOTHO: Woman carrying water.

EGGS COOKED IN TOMATOES

4 small tomatoes
4 eggs
2 tbls. oil or shortening
1 small onion, finely chopped
½ cup water

Wash tomatoes and cut a slice off the top of each. Carefully scoop out the pulp with a teaspoon; save pulp. Break an egg into each tomato. Add salt and pepper to taste. Fry chopped onion in hot oil. Add tomato pulp and water; boil. When boiling starts, place tomatoes with eggs in the sauce. Cover saucepan and cook until the eggs have set (about 10 minutes). Serves 4.

EGG RISSOLES

4 eggs
½ cup milk
¼ cup flour
2 small carrots, chopped
2 leaves spinach (1 cup), chopped
1 medium onion, chopped
¼ cup oil or shortening

Hard-boil two of the eggs for 10 minutes. Break the remaining 2 eggs in a bowl. Add milk and flour to the bowl and mix thoroughly, using egg beater or fork. Clean, peel and cut up vegetables finely, add to flour mixture. Shell hard-boiled eggs; chop finely and add to mixture. Add salt and pepper to taste. Drop mixture in spoonfuls into hot oil. Fry until light brown. Serve hot. Serves 4.

EGGPLANT AND POTATO STEW

1 lb. eggplant (1 medium)
2 medium onions, chopped
¼ cup oil or shortening

curry powder
4 large potatoes
2 cups boiling water
3 tbls. mealie meal (cornmeal)
2 tbls. tomato sauce
1 egg

Chop onions; fry in hot oil until light brown. Wash and cut eggplant into 1 inch cubes. Add eggplant and curry powder to taste to the fried onion. Salt and pepper to taste. Cook slowly for 20 minutes. Wash, peel, and cut potatoes into cubes. Add to the stew, together with boiling water. When the potatoes are tender (20-40 minutes), sprinkle in the mealie meal. Boil for another 10 minutes. Add tomato sauce and beaten egg (this enriches and improves flavor) and boil for 5 minutes. Serves 5-6.

FISH CAKES

¼ cup flour ͻ · breadcrumbs
1 egg
¼ cup water or milk
½ lb. fileted fish
1 medium onion, chopped
2 tbls. oil or shortening

Mix flour, egg and water or milk into a batter. Cut fish into small pieces and add to batter with salt and pepper to taste. Chop onion and add to mixture. Fry spoonfuls of mixture in hot oil until well-browned on all sides. Serves 2.

LESOTHO SCONES

2 cups flour
¼ tsp. salt
1½ tsp. baking powder
½ cup butter

2 tsp. sugar
1 egg
milk or water (about 2 tbls.)

Sift flour, salt and baking powder together. Rub batter into flour until no lumps are left. Mix in sugar. Beat egg; mix with flour and butter, using a fork, add milk or water until a soft, slightly sticky dough is formed. Roll out on a floured table to the thickness of a finger. Cut out scones with a cutter or glass. Bake on a greased baking sheet in a moderate oven (350 degrees) for 15-20 minutes. For a richer scone mixture, more than 1 egg may be used, and cinnamon may be added if desired. Makes 30.

MEALIE MEAL SALAD

1½ cups mealie meal (corn meal)
4 cups water
2 carrots, chopped
2 eggs
1 medium onion, chopped
2 tomatoes, chopped

Add mealie meal to boiling water and stir until smooth. Cook for 10 minutes, remove from heat to cool. Boil carrots and eggs together. Shell eggs. Chop eggs and vegetables finely. Add to meal paste; season with salt and pepper to taste. Serve cold, with mayonnaise as a dressing. Serves 5.

MEAT STEW (Traditional)

1 lb. meat
4 cups water
2 small onions, diced
2 small carrots, diced
2 large potatoes, diced
¼ cup flour
curry powder

Cut meat into pieces. Cook in water until tender (about 1 hour). Wash, peel and dice vegetables. Add to the meat; cover and cook for 30 minutes. Stir in flour, curry powder; salt and pepper to taste. Cook slowly for 5 minutes or more. To increase the quantity of this stew, serve with gravy. Also, cereals and other vegetables may be added as a variation. Serves 4.

MIXED CEREAL RISSOLES

½ lb. wheat, sorghum, and corn (about 1/3 cup each)
5 cups water
1 medium onion, chopped
1 egg
1 tbls. flour
2 tbls. oil or shortening

Wash and soak wheat, sorghum and corn overnight. Boil until tender in the same water (about 45 minutes). Grind or mince mixture into a soft dough. Add finely chopped onions, egg, flour; salt and pepper to taste. Mix well. Turn out onto a floured board or table. Shape into cakes; brown in very hot oil. Serves 6.

MIXED CEREAL STEW

4 cups water
½ cup sorghum
½ cup wheat
2 tbls. oil or shortening
1 small onion, sliced
½ cup milk

Clean and soak sorghum and wheat overnight. Boil cereals in the same water until soft (about 45 minutes). In a large pan, fry onion in hot oil until light brown. Add cereals and milk to the fried onion. Boil for 5 minutes. Add salt and pepper to taste and serve. Serves 4.

MIXED VEGETABLE RISSOLES

1 cup flour or breadcrumbs
2 eggs
1 cup milk
2 medium onions, chopped
1 cup vegetables, in season
½ cup oil or shortening

Make a batter from flour, eggs and milk. Add salt and pepper to taste. Clean vegetables; chop leafy vegetables and grate root vegetables. Add to batter. Fry spoonfuls of the mixture in hot oil until brown on all sides. Serves 4.

___

Note: In Lesotho, the most commonly used vegetables are eggplant, lucerne, spinach, potatoes, carrots, and all leafy vegetables.

PUMPKIN PUDDING

12 ozs. canned pumpkin
1 cup milk
2 tbls. sugar
2 eggs

Add sugar and milk to pumpkin in saucepan. Bring to a boil. Beat yolk of eggs. Stir pumpkin mixture into beaten yolks. Beat the whites stiffly and fold into mixture. Serves 4.

PUMPKIN STEW

1 small onion, sliced
1 lb. canned pumpkin
2 tbls. oil or shortening

Peel, and slice onion. Cook pumpkin and onion in heated oil for about 10 minutes. Add 1/2 cup water, if necessary; salt and pepper to taste. Cook slowly for about 10 minutes more. Serves 4.

STUFFED CABBAGE

1 medium cabbage
3 tbls. oil or shortening
2 medium onions, chopped
2/3 cup mealie meal (corn meal)
curry powder
1-3 medium tomatoes, chopped

Remove the thick outer layers of the cabbage with a knife. Soften them by putting them in boiling water for a few minutes until they are pliable. Fry onion in half the quantity of oil until light brown. Add mealie meal and stir well. Add curry powder, salt, and pepper to taste. Wrap this mixture in each of the softened leaves. Tie them with clean string or use toothpicks to secure. Wash and chop the rest of the cabbage. Fry in remaining oil. Add stuffed leaves and enough water to cover them. Steam over gentle heat until most of the liquid has evaporated. Add chopped tomatoes, salt, pepper, and curry powder to taste. Cook for few minutes more. Serves 6.

Note: Instead of mealie meal, rice or breadcrumbs may be used. Eggs may be added to make this dish more nutritious.

TOMATO SOUP

1 small onion, chopped
1 small carrot, chopped
2 tbls. oil or shortening
2 tbls. flour
4 cups hot water
4 medium tomatoes, chopped
1 tsp. sugar

Wash onion and carrot; chop finely and fry in oil. Steam for 10 minutes. Stir in flour, water, chopped tomatoes, and sugar. Salt and pepper to taste. Stir well and simmer for 10 more minutes. Serves 4.

LIBERIA

Ever since Liberia was founded in 1821 for the resettling of freed Black people from the United States, the majority of the people in Liberia have engaged in the cultivation of their own rice, sugar cane and cassava. Rice is the staple food of Liberia and is eaten at least twice a day. Fufu is a popular dish eaten with highly seasoned soup.

Suggested Menu Plan:
Lunch: Cassava Leaf and Rice
Dinner: Jollof Rice

CASSAVA LEAF

> 1 lb. beef
> 1 small stock fish
> 4 bonnies (small very bony fish)
> 2 dried fish
> 2 onions, ground
> 3 cups cassava leaf
> 3 cups palm oil
> 2 pods hot pepper (optional)

Boil meat, stock fish and bonnies until tender. Add dried fish and ground onions and steam until about 2 cups of liquid remain in the pan. Steam cassava leaves and wash. Grind in mortar or meat grinder. (Grind with hot pepper, if desired.) Add cassava leaf to fish and meat and boil for about 25 minutes, or until there is hardly any liquid left. Add palm oil; cook until all liquid is removed. Serve on steaming hot rice. Serves 4.

LIBERIA: Poro Mask, wood, metal, hair and movable jaw, Ge Tribe.

GINGER BEER

25 pieces ginger
2 pineapples, unpeeled and cut into chunks
2 tsp. yeast (optional)
1 gal. boiling water
3½ cups molasses

Beat ginger pieces. Add pineapple with peeling and yeast, if desired. Pour boiling water over this and let stand overnight. The following day, strain. Add molasses; chill and serve. Ginger beer may be diluted with water if too strong. Extra sugar or ginger may be added if desired.

GOAT SOUP

2 lbs. goat meat
hot peppers
2 medium onions, sliced
2 qts. water
3 fresh tomatoes
1 tbls. tomato paste

Cut up goat meat into 2-3 inch pieces. Wash well and season with hot peppers, salt and black pepper to taste. Cover with sliced onions. Let stand for 1 hour to allow seasoning to soak in. Add water and boil until meat is tender. Add fresh tomatoes, tomato paste, and more water if desired. Continue cooking until tomatoes are soft. Serve very hot. Serves 6.

JOLLOF RICE

1 lb. chicken
½ lb. stewing beef
½ lb. smoked ham or bacon

½ cup oil or shortening
2 onions, sliced
1 Liberian pepper, sliced (optional)
½ can 3 oz. tomato paste
1½ lbs. cabbage, cut into wedges
1½ cups rice
6 cups water

Cut chicken, beef and ham or bacon into 1-2 inch chunks. Season with salt and black pepper to taste. Flour and fry in hot oil. Drain oil into Dutch oven or heavy-bottomed pot. Sauté sliced onions and sliced Liberian pepper, if desired. Add meat and tomato paste and stir well. If chicken is tough, it may be added at this time. Add water and taste for seasoning. Cover, bring to a boil and cook over low heat for 10 minutes. Add chicken, if you have not done so already, and rice. As soon as this mixture starts to boil, stir and reduce flame to lowest heat. Add cabbage wedges and cook until rice is loose and fluffy, not soggy. Stir often to prevent sticking. Serves 6.

RICE BREAD

2 cups cream of rice
3 tbls. sugar
4 tsp. baking powder
½ tsp. salt
1½ mashed plantains or bananas
2 eggs
1½ cups milk
1 cup oil

Mix dry ingredients. Gradually add plantains or bananas, eggs, and milk. Add oil and blend thoroughly. Bake in a well-greased 8" x 12" pan at 375 degrees for 45 minutes or until a dry fork stuck in the center comes out clean.

MALAGASY REPUBLIC

Although the island of Madagascar (Malagasy Republic) is less than 250 miles from the mainland of Africa, the Malagasy people are ethnically and economically isolated from the other Africans, and their strongest ties are probably with Ceylon and India. The balance of crops grown for consumption at home versus crops for exporting is presently at a good level. The government is now involved in producing incentive for the average farmer to grow rich crops for export, like coffee, vanilla and cloves; hitherto the average farmer has been completely happy if he could grow just enough rice and raise just enough cattle to feed and clothe his family. Rice is the basic food, supplemented by cassava and corn.

Suggested Menu Plan:

Lunch: Soup à la Malgache and crackers or bread

Dinner: Tomatoes Rougaille, Curried Chicken Malagasy, fruit

CURRIED CHICKEN MALAGASY

3-4 lbs. frying chicken
½ cup oil or shortening
½ cup onion, finely minced
1 clove garlic, minced
1 tbls. curry powder
2 cups tomatoes, coarsely diced
2 cups hot water
2 tbls. salt
1-6 oz. can evaporated milk
2 tbls. flour

Have your butcher cut the chicken into serving-size pieces. Heat oil in a heavy skillet over moderate heat. Add onion, garlic, and curry powder. Cook for about 5 minutes, stirring gently. Add chicken; brown on both sides. Remove chicken and keep warm. Add tomatoes to oil in the frying pan and cook for about 3 minutes, stirring constantly. Add hot water and salt; stir long enough to mix thoroughly. Return chicken to pan; simmer until tender (about 50 minutes). Remove chicken to hot serving platter. You will probably have about 2 cups of liquid left in the pan. Blend together evaporated milk and flour and add to liquid, stirring constantly. Continue to cook and stir until liquid thickens. This dish may be accompanied by *Tomatoes Rougaille* (see p. 77). Serves 6.

SOUP À LA MALGACHE

3 lbs. veal bones
2 tbls. salt
2 qts. water
2 large tomatoes, peeled and diced
3 medium potatoes, peeled and diced
3 carrots, peeled and diced
1 small turnip, peeled and diced

1 leek (optional)
1 cup string beans (optional)

Place veal bones in a 5-quart saucepan; add water and salt. Bring to a boil and simmer for 1 hour. Add tomatoes and onions and simmer for another 1½ hours. Add remainder of vegetables and simmer until vegetables are tender (about 1 hour). Remove vegetables with a sieve; return veal bones to the broth. Serves 6.

TOMATOES ROUGAILLE
1 cup green peppers, finely diced
2 cups raw tomatoes, finely diced
2 tbls. water
1 tsp. salt
few drops Tabasco sauce

Combine green peppers and tomatoes. Blend together water, Tabasco sauce and salt; stir lightly into the blended vegetables. Serve with *Curried Chicken Malagasy* (see p. 76). Serves 6.

VARENGA (Shredded Chuck)

2 lbs. boneless chuck beef cut into small pieces
water
2 tbls. salt
1 clove garlic
1 onion, sliced

Place beef in a 2-quart saucepan; cover with water. Add salt, garlic and onion. Cover; bring to a boil and simmer for 2 hours, or until the meat can be shredded with a fork. Add more water if necessary during the cooking period. When the meat is tender, strain and shred. Transfer to a 7" x 11" baking dish and roast at 400 degrees for 1/2 hour or until meat is browned. Serves 6.

MALI

Millet and rice are Mali's principal crops; in fact, the country grows enough rice to supply her own population and most of neighboring Senegal's. (Senegal does not have the climatic conditions for rice.) The railroad system in Mali, a land-locked nation, is being improved for transportation of crops as well as valuable minerals.

Suggested Menu Plan:

Dinner: Chicken and Sauce, Rice, Mint Tea
         (see Morocco section)

CHICKEN AND SAUCE

4-6 lbs. frying chicken	½ head cabbage
½ cup oil or shortening	few pieces of eggplant
1 large onion, diced	2 carrots, sliced
2 tomatoes, peeled and diced	5 small fresh okra
1½ tbls. tomato paste	1 small bay leaf
4 cups water	

Cut chicken into pieces for frying. Season with salt and pepper to taste. Cook in oil on a low flame together with onion. When onion starts to brown, add tomatoes and tomato paste diluted with 1/2 tsp. water. Stir occasionally. When chicken is browned all over, add water. Bring to a boil; add cabbage, eggplant, carrots, okra, and bay leaf. Let simmer until fully cooked (about 1-1 1/2 hours). Before serving, thicken the sauce with corn or wheat flour diluted with water. Serve hot with white rice. Serves 4-5.

MALI: cloth being dyed.

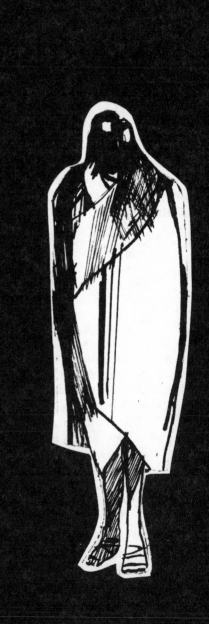

MAURITANIA

Mauritania is a sparsely populated part of the Sahara. Its northern Moors, comprising about 75 to 80 per cent of its population, are mainly nomadic pastoralists. The tribes of the south depend upon the production of grains along the banks of Senegal.

Suggested Menu Plan:

Lunch: Brochettes and Mint Tea

BROCHETTES

    1 cup oil or shortening
    2 red pimentos
    2 mutton livers
    2 mutton hearts
    1 lb. breaded lamb

Crush pimentos and mix with oil. On each barbecue skewer, put a piece of liver, a piece of heart, a piece of breaded lamb, etc. Dip each skewer into oil and pimento mixture. Grill over the barbecue. Serve with tomato sauce flavoured with pimento, or a spiced barbecue sauce. For full flavor, it is best to grill the meat for only a short time. Serves 4.

MAURITANIAN TEA CEREMONY

Mint tea is the universal drink of North Africa, and in Mauritania, whether in the most fashionable home or the most modest tent, the mint tea ceremony is the most important welcoming procedure for any reception. The ceremony of mysterious origin is practiced according to traditions handed down from generation to generation, and religiously observed to the letter in every household. The unchangeable customs require that the tea be served three times, in three different ways, with three characteristic tastes:

1. slightly sour
2. sweeter and slightly flavoured with mint
3. real syrup of mint and tea

In many cases, the time required for making and drinking the tea is an indication of the degree of regard one has towards one's guest, as in certain tribes the tradition demands that the "reunion" end after drinking the third glass.

Preparation and Servings

top grade green China tea
22 lumps cane sugar
fresh mint, if not available, dried mint

Put water on to boil. Pour 3/4 cup tea into a tin tea-pot. "Rinse" the tea by pouring a small amount of boiling water into the tea pot and then emptying the water into another container. Put 5 lumps of sugar into the tea pot and fill with boiling water. Shake the tea pot from right to left and empty the contents into 5 tea glasses (for 4 guests), which are the size of a large liquor glass. In the beginning keep the tea-pot very close to the glasses, then, while filling each glass three-quarters full, slowly lift the tea-pot up to 20-25 inches. This process is part of the ritual and has the effect of airing the perfumed liquid. Pour the glasses back into the tea-pot and heat until boiling. At this stage of preparation, the person making the liquid tastes it. If more tea or sugar is desired, he adds it, and repeats the procedure of shaking the tea and filling the glasses until the tea is ready.

For the second glass, throw a pinch more of tea, some mint leaves, and 7 lumps of sugar into the tea pot. Fill with boiling water, shake, and proceed as in the first cup with pouring and tasting.

For the third and final glass, throw into the tea-pot a pinch of tea, some mint leaves (more than the quantity of the second glass) and 10 lumps of sugar. Fill with boiling water and repeat procedure as in the first cup.

MOROCCO

Morocco is mainly an agricultural and pastoral country separated from Europe by the thin Strait of Gibraltar. Its chief agricultural products are barley, wheat, and corn. During meals plain water or orange juice is served. On very special occasions almond milk or Turkish coffee may be served in very small cups or glasses. But Mint Tea is served always before, during, and after dinner. Morocco ranks first throughout the world in phosphate exports. It produces 10% of the world's cobalt. In addition, Morocco has an allure for the tourist and has developed a sizable tourist industry.

Suggested Menu Plan:

Dinner: Couscous and Stew, Mint Tea

COUSCOUS AND STEW

2 lbs. Couscous*	2 quarts water
2 lbs. lamb (shoulder or cutlets) or chicken	1½ cups chick peas (cooked or canned)
2 large onions, quartered	1 pkg. carrots
tumeric, saffron, ginger (to taste)	3 turnips
	3 zucchini
salt and pepper	1 small cabbage (optional)
1 cup oil	1 cup seedless raisins
½ cube butter	(optional)

*COUSCOUS GRAIN: this may be made by rolling semolina with very little water by hand. A couscous pot should be used; otherwise use a large pot with a colander which fits exactly on top of the pot.

MOROCCO: Sedjenane Pottery Designs applied with vegetable juices.

Put meat, onions, spices, oil and butter into a pot with water. Boil for one hour or until meat is tender and comes off the bones easily. Add chick peas. Put couscous in colander (use cheese cloth at bottom if holes are too large). Put under faucet and run cold water over grain. Drain for 20 minutes. Put colander on top of pot to steam. After 15-20 minutes remove couscous from colander and place in a large dish. Add salt dissolved in a little water and add one cup oil, little by little, mixing well with hands or fork. It must not be lumpy; separate the grains. Put couscous back in colander and place on top of pot. Total steaming time should be at least 1/2 hour or longer. Add vegetables and raisins to broth. Cooking time will depend on how firm you like the vegetables. Serving: Place couscous in the center of a large dish and add butter. Mix well to make a cone-shaped mass. Place vegetables around cone with meat on top. Pour broth over all, little by little, to make it neither soggy nor dry. For a spicier flavor a separate sauce may be prepared with 2 cups broth, 3 tsp. paprika, and a big pinch of red cayenne pepper well mixed with a fork. Serves 6-8.

DJAJ M'KALLI (Chicken with Lemons and Olives)

3 whole chickens
6 cloves garlic, crushed
2 tbls. salt
(Marinade Ingredients)
3/4 cup vegetable oil
2 tsp. ginger
1 tsp. tumeric
1 tsp. black pepper
pinch of saffron
salt

(Stewing Ingredients)
3 medium onions, grated
1 stick butter
2 cloves garlic, chopped
1 quart water
1/2 jar Greek Kalamate olives
2 pickled lemons
(wash off brine)*

Clean and remove all fat from chickens. Rub with mixture of garlic and salt. Put in a large pot and cover with water. Let stand for one hour, then remove chickens from water. Rub chickens with marinade ingredients. Allow to marinate for a few hours or overnight in the refrigerator. To cook, place chicken in a pot and add onions, butter, garlic, and water. Bring to a boil, then simmer until tender. When almost done, add olives and pickled lemons.* When chickens are tender, remove from pot and boil down sauce until fairly thick. Return chickens to pot and reheat before serving. Serves 6-8.

MINT TEA (Serve always before, during and after dinner)

China green tea
fresh mint (one tsp. rose water can be substituted for fresh mint)
sugar (24 cubes)

Rinse a six-cup teapot with fresh boiling water to warm it. Pour out water. Put one tablespoon tea in pot. Pour 1/4 cup boiling water over tea to rinse it, and pour out water. Add sugar, preferably in cubes (about 24). Fill pot with boiling water. Add one handful of fresh mint, stirring immediately with spoon so that leaves do not float on surface. Let stand two minutes, then serve in small glasses. Serves 6.

Note: There is a more complete explanation of the North African tea ceremony with a slightly different recipe on p. 82.

*PICKLED LEMONS (Must be made at least two weeks before using)

Quarter lemons, leaving one end attached. Fill with salt and put in glass or stoneware jar with tight lid. Put in as many lemons as will fit snugly. Let stand for *at least two weeks.*

NIGERIA

Nigeria substantially contributes to the world market with her exports of cola nuts, cocoa, and palm oil from the south, and peanuts and cotton from the north, and, in addition, oil has been recently discovered. Plants in jungle clearings provide the major source of nutrition for the local population; more than 150 varieties of local fish are also an important source of protein. The staple foods are starches: roots (yams and cassava) and cereals (corn and millet). Native beers may be brewed from corn, sorghum, palm sap, or sugar cane.

Suggested Menu Plan:

Lunch: Spinach Soup, Agidi

Dinner: Salad, Moyinmoyin, Agidi

AGIDI (Cornstarch Porridge)

1 cup corn starch
6 tbls. cold milk or 4 tbls. cream diluted with 2 tbls. water
8 cups boiling water

For the *Agidi* to be properly solidified, it is wise to prepare it about four hours before serving time. Pour boiling water into the paste of cornstarch and milk until the paste gradually congeals, stirring simultaneously. Smooth out and pour *Agidi* into a clean bowl. Cover the bowl and cool (though not in the icebox). Serve cold with *Efo* (see p. 90). Serves 4.

NIGERIA: Meko Gelede masquerader.

COOKED EGGPLANT APPETIZER

1 large eggplant
1 tsp. mashed sesame seeds
½ tsp. salt
1 clove garlic, mashed
juice of 1 lemon (4 tbls.)
2 tbls. parsley

Peel eggplant and bake or steam until tender (about 10-15 minutes). Mash with a wooden spoon. Add the sesame paste, salt, garlic, and lemon juice. Beat until smooth. Mound on a shallow dish and sprinkle with chopped parsley. Serve with pieces of flat, round, Arabian bread. Serves 4.

CURRY DIP FOR RAW CAULIFLOWER

1 cup mayonnaise
3 tbls. chili sauce
2 tbls. curry powder
1 tbls. worchestershire sauce
1 tsp. onion juice
1 clove garlic
salt and pepper

Mix all seasoning with mayonnaise. Salt and pepper to taste. Chill. Serve with raw cauliflower sprouts, or other pieces of raw vegetables.

EFO (Spinach Soup)

1 lb. fish or meat
3 cups water
1 ½ lbs. fresh spinach, finely cut
1 large onion, diced
2 tomatoes, diced
½ lb. shrimp

¼ cup palm oil
pinch of salt
dash of thyme
½ tsp. of crushed pepper

Cut meat or fish into small pieces. Add water, salt to taste and boil until tender, permitting water to evaporate completely. While meat or fish is cooking, wash spinach thoroughly and cut finely. Dice onions and tomatoes. Clean and cut shrimps. After the water has totally evaporated, add palm oil, onion, tomatoes, salt, thyme, and pepper, and cook over a moderate heat for 5 minutes. Then add spinach and shrimps and continue cooking, adding no water, until done (about 20 minutes). Don't overcook. Serve with hot *Agidi* (see p. 109). Serves 4.

MOYINMOYIN OR ELELE (Bean Pudding)

1 ½ cups black-eyed peas (white beans)
1 medium onion, ground
3 tbls. palm oil
1 large tomato
3 tbls. shrimp
dash of garlic salt
½ tsp. curry powder
1 tsp. ground red pepper
1 ½ cups hot water

Moyinmoyin may be classified as a pudding made out of black-eyed peas (white beans). Soak beans overnight if *moyinmoyin* is to be eaten for lunch the next day. Remove hulls of peas. Clean peas and grind very fine. Grind onion, shrimps, and tomato and mix well with ground peas. Add salt to taste, oil, dash of garlic, curry powder, red pepper and hot water. Mix and blend well, taste again for salt, then pour preparation into six small or medium-sized custard cups, well-greased beforehand. Set cups in cooking pot, add water to well cover bottom of pot. Cover and cook over medium heat until solidified. Eat warm or allow to cool. Serve traditionally with *Agidi* (see p. 89), as a meal in itself, or accompanied with green salad. Serves 6.

SENEGAL

Senegal, independent since 1960, is the most westernized part of the former French West Africa. Peanuts are still the main export; after World War II the improvement of mineral fertilizers and selected seeding processes saved the soil from the disasters previously inevitable in a one-crop country. As you will gather from the Senegalase recipes, their main diet consists of rice and smoked fish, cooked with vegetables, palm oil, and hot pepper. The spice used in many recipes, netetou, is indigenous to Senegal; the closest substitute is curry.

Suggested Menu Plan:

Lunch: Yassa au Poisson, White Rice

Dinner: Salad, Fish Stew and Peanuts

CALDOU (Sauce to Accompany Rice)

    2 cups water
    1 lb. very small fish
    1 small onion, sliced
    1 large red pepper, sliced
    1-2 tbls. palm oil
    juice of 2 lemons (about ½ cup)

Heat water in saucepan and add cleaned fish, sliced onion, red pepper, oil and salt to taste. Boil on medium heat for 30 minutes. Remove from heat and mix in lemon juice. Serve as a side dish for white rice. Serves 3.

CAMBAGNY AU NETETOU GRILLE
(Fish with Netetou and Rice)

tail end of thiof (false cod)
3" square dried fish
4 oz. netetou
1 small red pepper
1 large onion
4 1/3 cups rice
1 ½ oz. dried shrimps
1 tbls. dried red pepper
1 tbls. salt
½ cup palm oil

Bring 8 cups of water to simmering. Add fish tail, dried fish, salt to taste, and a paste made of 1 oz. crushed netetou, red pepper, and onion. Cook for 1/2 hour. Remove fish and add washed rice to water. Stir well and cover. When water has evaporated, turn flame down to medium low. Put remainder of netetou in a frying pan and stir over heat until it starts to steam; pour it immediately into a mortar with shrimps and dried red pepper. Crush into a thin powder, adding salt. Remove rice from heat and serve with netetou powder, palm oil, and fish. Serves 4.

FOUFOU (Foufou with Fish)

4 1/3 cups flour
1 tbls. salt
10 cups water
1 ½ oz. netetou
1 large red pepper
4 small onions
1 cup palm oil
½ (head part) thiof (false cod) or diarogne (gilt-head)
2 ¼ lbs. fresh gombos (okra)
3" square cut of dried fish

Mix 2 cups flour with salt and 2 cups water. Stir over medium heat until boiling. Add remaining flour, stirring continuously to avoid lumping. Remove from heat when thick. Crush netetou, red peppers and onions; add palm oil. Heat this mixture and add fish head to it. Salt to taste. Simmer for 1-2 minutes, then add 8 cups water. Wash and thinly slice gombos. Drop into palm oil sauce with washed, dried fish. Bring to a boil, and when the gombos are cooked, remove fish and whip gombos. Return fish to the whipped sauce and pour into a soup tureen to serve. Serve flour paste separately. Serves 4-5.

Note: "Foufou à la viande (meat foufou using 1/2 lb. meat)" is prepared exactly like this "Foufou au poisson" except that when the gombos are whipped, the meat is not withdrawn. When you cannot find fresh gombos (okra), use dried gombo-powder if available. Cook with fish and after fish has been removed, whip sauce until firm and thick.

GAR

    I large onion
    2 cups palm oil
    18 cherry (tiny) tomatoes
    ½ (head part) diarogne (gilt-head) or thiof (false cod)
    12 cups water
    3" square of dried fish
    2 large red peppers, sliced
    4-1/3 lbs. semolina (hard wheat) or 8¾ cups rice,
       pre-cooked

Fry sliced onion in 1/4 cup palm oil. Remove seeds from tomatoes, mash and spread over onions with fish and salt to taste. Let simmer for 1-2 minutes, then add remainder of palm oil, 12 cups water, dried fish, red peppers. Cook until fish is done; remove fish. Stir the cooked semolina or rice into the sauce little by little, and heat for 15 minutes. Spread melted butter on top and serve with fish. Serves 8.

M'BAKHAL AUX ARACHIDES (Fish Stew and Peanuts)

½ (head part) thiof (false cod)
2" square of dried fish
4 oz. netetou
2 large red peppers
1 large onion
4 1/3 cups rice
3 cups shelled peanuts, crushed
7 tbls. butter
couscousiere

In the bottom part of the double boiler, boil thiof, fish, and a paste made from 1 oz. crushed netetou, 1 red pepper and the onion with 8 cups water. Salt to taste. Put the rice in the couscousiere and place on the boiling stew. After the stew is cooked (30-45 minutes), remove fish from stew and dump rice into stew. Stir well and cover. After water has evaporated, lower heat and sprinkle rice with crushed peanuts. Cover pot again. Crush remaining netetou, red pepper, and salt to taste into a paste. Make a well in the rice in the pot and pour the paste into it but *do not mix*. Cook, for a few minutes over medium heat and spoon out the netetou paste. Serve rice sprinkled with netetou paste and melted butter and fish. Serves 8.

SOUPIKANDIA (RIZ À LA SAUCE GOMBO)
(Fish and Okra Sauce)

8 small onions
2 large red peppers
1½ oz. netetou
2 cups palm oil
½ (tail end) diarogne (gilt-head)
3" square of dried fish
1 lb. fresh gombo (okra)

Peel and slice onions. Crush with red peppers and netetou in a mortar. Heat palm oil in a saucepan, and add crushed mixture, fish tail and salt to taste. Let simmer 1-2 minutes, then add 12 cups water. Wash dried fish, and add to sauce with washed and sliced gombos. Boil over medium heat for 45 minutes. Withdraw fish and stir in gombo powder. When sauce thickens, return fish to pan and taste for salt. Simmer for a few more minutes and serve with rice. Serves 4-5.

TIEP AU DIENG (Fish and Rice)

2 lbs. rice (or enough for 6 people)
6 fish—diagrone (gilt-head) or thiof (cod)
6 onions, sliced
4 tomatoes, chopped
2 hot peppers, chopped
1 head cabbage, shredded
6 carrots, sliced or strips
½ lb. gombo (okra), cut up
½ lb. manioc
1 eggplant
3 turnips, sliced
salt and pepper

Boil rice for 30 minutes or follow the direction if using instant rice. In a separate pot, boil the fish for 15-20 minutes or until ready. Do not cut up fish, let each person take their own portion when served.

In a third pot brown chopped onions, tomatoes, and hot peppers. When brown, add oil and other vegetables. If water is necessary to help make a sauce, add water from the boiled fish. Simmer vegetables for 15 minutes. Salt and pepper to taste.

When vegetables are ready, put in a serving bowl and place the fish on top. Put the rice in a separate bowl and serve. Serves 6.

YASSA AU POISSON (Marinated Fish)

½ tsp. salt
¼ tsp. pepper
½ big red pepper, sliced
juice of 2 lemons (about ½ cup)
2 tbls. vinegar
½ cup palm oil
3 small gilt-heads or mullets, fresh
4 small onions, sliced

Mix salt, pepper, sliced red pepper, lemon juice, vinegar, and a few drops of oil together in a bowl. Heat 1/4 cup oil in a frying pan and fry washed fish over a very hot flame until browned. Fry the onions until brown in another pan with the rest of the oil. When browned, add marinating liquid, grilled fish and 1 1/2 cups water. Cover and let simmer on medium heat for 10 minutes. Serve with white rice. You will get the best results if this recipe is scrupulously timed. Serves 5.

SIERRA LEONE

Fufu (Cassava Balls, p. 103) is the staple food for the people of Sierra Leone, and the steady sound of the stick pounding cassava into pulp is the most familiar sound in the village. Fish dishes are quite popular; fresh fish are boiled or wrapped in leaves and baked, while dried fish is the preferred form for stews. We have only included a few recipes from Sierra Leone, because we found that the same foods were eaten in neighboring countries, like Ghana and Senegal. If your mother-in-law has just returned from Sierra Leone, and you want to impress her by preparing a dish that she probably enjoyed there, serve her Groundnut Soup (p. 46) or Caldou (p. 93).

SIERRA LEONE: Musician—Balangi with mallets and bells.

Suggested Menu Plan:

Breakfast: Fish and Coffee or Tea

Lunch: Caldou, Rice, Cassava Chips

Dinner: Groundnut Soup, Fufu

CASSAVA CHIPS

    1 large cassava or yam
    1 cup oil or shortening

    Peel cassava or yam and cut paper thin, using potato peeler. Fry in deep fat until golden brown. Drain on paper that has been sprinkled with salt. These can be kept for several days in a tight jar and can be reheated in oven.

FUFU (Cassava Balls)

1 large cassava or yam
1 egg
5 tbls. evaporated milk
1 onion, grated
pinch of garlic salt
3 tbls. butter or margarine

Peel and cut cassava or yam into small pieces. Boil until tender (about 20 minutes) using half as much water as vegetable in the pan. Drain off water and mash until smooth and fine. Add egg, milk, onion, and garlic salt; salt and pepper to taste. Beat and roll into 2-inch balls. If the mixture is too wet, add a little flour. Fry in butter until brown. Makes 8.

SOMALIA

The Somalians are mainly nomadic people who depend on camels and sheep for their livelihood. Two-thirds of the population is engaged in raising livestock and tanning hides; those engaged in agriculture cultivate bananas, the main export, chiefly for Italy. According to legend, Somalia is the country where the Wise Men of the Bible gathered the frankincense and myrrh for their presents to the Holy Child.

Suggested Menu Plan:

Breakfast: Papaya and Tea

Lunch: Moushkaki

Dinner: Vegetable Curry with Meat or Meat Curry
with Rice, fruit in season (e.g. mangoes), Tea

BASIC RECIPE FOR CURRY

It is often thought that curry is a dish in itself, or a means of finishing up cooked food, but rather it is a way of preparing food with certain spices and herbs to accentuate rather than to smother the flavor. Almost anything fresh can be curried: every edible fish or fowl, all kinds of meat, vegetables, and even eggs. Of course, whatever it is should be worth the time and trouble necessary. A curry dish can be made, and in fact will taste better if it is made, the day before it is to be eaten.

3 tbls. oil
½ cup onion
3 tbls. flour
2 tsp. cumin
½ tsp. ginger
¼ tsp. red pepper
1 tsp. salt
1 ½ tsp. coriander
½ tsp. tumeric
1 tsp. black pepper
¼ tsp. cloves
½ tsp. cinnamon
2 tsp. curry powder
grated lemon rind and juice
2 cups liquid
2 cups chopped meat, fish, or vegetables

Brown onions in hot oil. Mix all dry spices and add to onions. Cook three minutes over low heat to remove the raw taste of the spices, stirring constantly. Add rind and juice plus 2 cups liquid. (This may be stock, water with chicken bouillon cubes, or for shrimp curry, coconut milk is delicious.) Simmer until it thickens slightly. Add cooked, cut-up meat, chicken, fish or vegetables. Freezes well if prepared ahead of time. Serve meat or fish curry with rice, vegetable curry with meat. Serves 6.

COOKED MANGOES

6 mangoes
1 coconut
2-3 tbls. sugar
ground coriander (gorje)
split coriander seeds (heil)
dash of cinnamon

Wash mangoes but do not peel; slice down either side of the stone, thus cutting each mango into three pieces. Put all pieces into a saucepan. Prepare coconut milk by grating coconut meat and then tying it in a piece of clean muslin cloth. Squeeze muslin bag over a bowl to extract more juice from the coconut. Repeat the dipping process until all juice has been extracted and the water in the second bowl looks like thin milk. Discard coconut pulp. Pour the bowl with the thin milk into a saucepan with the mangoes. Boil and simmer until mangoes are cooked, i.e. when skins are tender. Then add to the thick milk sugar, cinnamon and split coriander seeds. Cover with lid and leave all to simmer until sauce thickens. Cool. Serves 6.

MASALA (Meat and Spiced Coconut)

¼ grated coconut
½ inch piece of green ginger
2 cloves garlic
½ tsp. saffron powder
1 tsp. coriander seeds
1 tsp. cumin seeds
2-3 red peppers
6 peppercorns
2 tbls. oil (ghee) or shortening
2 cinnamon sticks
2 cloves
2 cardamon pods
1 lb. minced meat
2 medium tomatoes, chopped

1 medium onion, sliced
1 cup peanuts
½ cup water

Grind together coconut, ginger, garlic, saffron, coriander, cumin seeds and peppers, adding a spoonful of water if necessary to make a smooth paste (called *masala*). Heat oil (*ghee*) and fry cinnamon, cloves, and cardamon pods for a minute in a covered pan. Add meat and brown well. Add finely chopped tomatoes, sliced onions, *masala* paste and peanuts. Add water and simmer until oil floats on top. Flavor with some chopped coriander and serve hot. Serves 4.

MOUSHKAKI (Barbecued Meat)

2 lbs. meat, cut into small cubes
crushed garlic (toon)
crushed ginger (zinjibil)
lemon juice, enough to cover meat
salt
black pepper
1 red pepper, chopped
3 onions, chopped
4 tomatoes, chopped
lettuce

Cut meat into small cubes of 1-2 inches square, 6-8 hours before serving. Put in a bowl and marinate using the garlic, ginger, lemon juice and salt and pepper to taste. When ready, put meat on skewers and cook over open charcoal. Serve with chopped onions, tomatoes, and lettuce, sprinkled with salt and lemon juice. Serves 4-6.

PAPAYA (Papaya Rings)

    1 large green (unripe) papaya
    1 coconut
    coriander seeds (heil)
    2-3 tbls. sugar

Skin papaya and cut into thin slices widthwise to form rings. Take out seeds from centers of rings. With a sharp knife, carefully cut each ring into spaghetti-like spirals by starting at the outside curve of the ring and going round and round until the center of the ring is reached. Prepare coconut milk by grating the coconut meat and tying it in a piece of clean muslin. Squeeze muslin bag over a bowl to extract the thick coconut milk. Take another basin and pour enough water into it to cover the papaya strips. Dip muslin bag in the water and squeeze lightly until all juice has been extracted from the coconut meat and the water looks like thin milk. Discard coconut pulp. Cover papaya spaghetti in saucepan with the second (thin) milk; boil and simmer gently until tender. If papaya needs to be stirred, push it around gently with a fork, or shake saucepan; too much stirring will break it up. When tender, add coriander seeds to taste, and sugar. Return all to fire and simmer until sauce thickens. Serve warm. Serves 6.

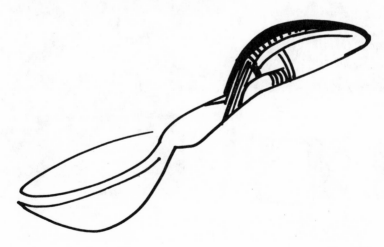

SUDAN

The Sudan with an area of 967,498 square miles is the largest of African countries. Sesame, cotton, and peanuts are grown in the Sudan for export, but almost all other crops (as well as large herds of livestock) are raised largely for subsistence. The basic food of the northern part of the country is millet (dura), while the South has optimum conditions for finger millet (eleusine) and maize.

Suggested Menu Plan:

Breakfast: Unleavened Bread and Coffee

Lunch: Lentil Sandwiches and Tea, Coconut Dessert

SUDAN: Compound.

COCONUT DESSERT

    1 coconut
    1 cup water
    2 tsp. gelatin
    2 eggs, separated
    3 tbls. sugar
    1 cup cream, whipped

Grate the coconut meat; add coconut to 1 cup water and boil for 20 minutes. Strain; this should make 3/4 cup of liquid. Dissolve the gelatin in the liquid. Beat egg yolks with sugar until well-blended. Slowly add gelatin and coconut to this. Refrigerate. When it begins to set, fold in the whipped cream. Refrigerate until this also has begun to set, and fold in beaten egg whites. Refrigerate until set. Good served with maraschino cherries. Serves 4-5.

LENTIL SANDWICHES

 ¾ cup lentils
 4 cups water
 1 tsp. lemon juice
 2 tsp. horseradish or spiced mustard
 1 tbls. butter, melted
 ¼ cup onion, minced
 12 slices bread
 chopped parsley

Boil lentils for 45-60 minutes, or until tender. Drain off water; mash. Add lemon juice, horseradish or spiced mustard, butter, and onions. Heat; salt and pepper to taste. Spread on slices of bread, preferably the flat, round Arabian loaves. Garnish with parsley. Serves 6.

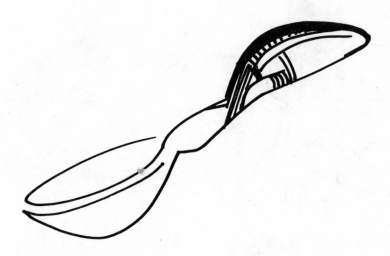

TUNISIA

The fertile soil of Tunisia produces an abundance of wheat, barley, oats, dates, apricots, almonds, figs, peaches, vegetables, and alfalfa grass. Livestock are raised extensively. The fishing industry along the Mediterranean Sea is being developed. The principal exports of Tunisia are olive oil, wine, grains, iron ore, lead and phosphate.

Suggested Menu Plan:

Breakfast: Lablabi and Turkish Coffee

Lunch: Kaftaji Djari and Watermelon

Dinner: Shakshouka, Tajeen, Plums, and Mint Tea

AKBAB (Braised Lamb)

1 lb. lamb
½ tsp. black pepper
1/3 cup olive oil
1 tsp. tomato paste
1 tsp. harissa
2 tbls. butter
1 small onion, finely chopped
bunch of parsley
juice of 1 small lemon (3 tbls.)

Cut meat into small pieces, season with black pepper and salt to taste; brown in hot oil for a few minutes. Add tomato paste and

TUNISIA: Detail of a Tunisian embroidery—Fish as Good Luck Symbol.

harissa. Cover with water and cook to desired doneness. When meat is ready, taste for seasoning. Add butter, mix and serve on individual plates. Sprinkle with a mixture of finely chopped onions, parsley and lemon juice. Serves 4.

BOUZA (Ice Cream)

>   2 cups sorghum flour
>   3 oz. shelled almonds
>   3 oz. shelled nuts
>   1¾ cups fresh milk, boiled
>   1 cup "castor" sugar (granulated)
>   1 oz. distilled geranium water

Sift flour. Add a little water, mix to a thick dough, and knead thoroughly. Add a further 2-2/3 cups water to the dough and put through a very fine sieve. Remove anything that will not go through the sieve and collect the liquid in a fairly large pan. Blanch the almonds by dipping them in boiling water for a few minutes. Roast with other nuts and remove skins from all. Add nuts, boiled milk, and sugar to dough. Heat, stirring until mixture achieves the consistency of thick cream. Add geranium water and serve.

COUSCOUS WITH LAMB

Couscous is probably the favorite dish of Tunisians. They can eat it all year round and sometimes more than once a week and not tire of its taste, since it tastes different according to whether it is prepared with lamb, chicken, fish, or vegetables. Made from fine semolina (or thickly-ground barley), *couscous* cannot be cooked directly over the flame, but requires its own utensil, the couscousiere (see Glossary, pp. 19-20). It is cooked using the steam of whatever it is prepared with.

>   ½ cup chick peas
>   1 slice lamb's tail fat ("liya")
>   1 lb. lamb

½ tbls. black pepper
½ cup olive oil
3-4 small onions
1 tbls. paprika
1 tbls. harissa
2-3 fresh tomatoes
3-4 potatoes
2-3 carrots
1 medium turnip
1½ lbs. couscous (fine grain preferably)
1 slice pumpkin
2-3 sweet peppers
a few hot peppers
2 tbls. salted butter
pinch of cinnamon
pinch of rose-bud powder
couscousiere

Soak chick peas overnight. Cut fat and meat into even pieces. Season with black pepper and salt, and brown in oil with 1 chopped onion in the bottom part of the double boiler. Add paprika, harissa diluted with a little water, sieved tomatoes, and chick peas. Prepare vegetables by peeling onions and potatoes and leaving them whole, by slicing the carrots in half, and by quartering the turnip. Add vegetables to meat and cover with 3 1/2 pints of water. Bring to a boil and reduce heat. Wet the couscous with a little fresh water, and put it in the couscousiere without packing the grains together. Fit into the lower part of the double boiler and cook for 30-40 minutes from the moment the steam starts rising through the couscous. Then remove the top of the boiler and empty couscous into a bowl. Sprinkle generously with fresh water and break up lumps of grain with a wooden spoon. This allows couscous to air and grains to separate.

Peel pumpkin, cut into slices and add it and the peppers to the sauce. Put top of boiler back on and cook for an additional 30 minutes over the steam. Empty couscous into large bowl. Using a ladle, skim the fat off the surface of the sauce and mix fat with butter and a pinch each of cinnamon and rose-bud water. Pour over couscous, mix thoroughly and arrange couscous evenly in the bowl. Check the sauce for seasoning and pour over couscous. Leave to stand for a short while and serve hot. Serves 6.

KAFTAJI DJARI (Meat Balls and Fried Vegetables)

½ lb. boned meat, minced
2 tsp. black pepper
2 tbls. tabil
1 slice liver, chopped
½ lb. fresh pumpkin
2-3 sweet peppers
a few hot peppers
3-4 potatoes
2/3 cup olive oil
4 eggs
3-4 fresh tomatoes
½ tbls. harissa
a few cloves of garlic
2 tbls. paprika

Mince meat and season with a pinch of black pepper and a pinch of tabil. Salt to taste and make balls the size of a large hazelnut. Chop liver into small pieces and season in the same manner. Peel pumpkin and cut into thin slices. Wash peppers, and with the point of a knife make an incision in the side of each one, big enough to allow you to put in a pinch of salt and a pinch of tabil. Cut potatoes into chips. Heat oil; fry meat balls, liver, pumpkin, peppers and potatoes. Fry eggs separately. Cut fried peppers lengthwise, remove seeds, and return to meat.

Make a sauce with sieved or crushed tomatoes and the remainder of the frying oil, adding harissa, crushed garlic, and a little water. Season with paprika, salt and tabil. Put 1-2 tablespoons of this sauce on each plate, a fried egg, and arrange the vegetables. Add fried meat balls and liver. Serves 4.

KHOBZ MBASSIS (Homemade Bread)

5½ lbs. fine semolina (hard wheat)
1 small slice of "liya" (lamb's tail fat)
1/3 cup olive oil
1 tbls. salt
7 oz. yeast
2 tbls. sesame seeds
1 tbls. green aniseed
1 egg

Heap semolina and make a well in the center. Melt the fat from the lamb's tail in the oil and pour this liquid into the center of the well. Dissolve salt in a little water, add to the mixture and knead the whole rapidly. Again make a well in the center, add yeast and pour about 4 1/2 cups of warm water over it gradually, mixing yeast well with water. Work dough energetically for 15-20 minutes until smooth. Cover with a cloth and allow to rise in a warm place for 1-1 1/2 hours until doubled in bulk. Sift seeds carefully and mix into dough. Knead again for 20-25 minutes. Divide dough into small loaves, shaping them according to your taste, and let rise. Brush with beaten egg and bake in oven at 400 degrees for 10 minutes; reduce heat to 375 degrees and bake for 35-40 minutes until a thick light crust is formed.

LABLABI (Pea Soup)

1 lb. chick peas (2 cups)
few cloves of garlic
1 tbls. harissa
1 tbls. cumin
juice of lemon (3 tbls.)
1/3 cup olive oil
few slices of one-day-old bread

Wash chick peas well and leave them overnight to soak. Cook in the same water until tender (about 10-15 minutes). Add a further 3 1/2 cups of water and heat again. Add harissa, garlic and

119

cumin seeds. Season with salt to taste. Stir and cook a few minutes longer. Add olive oil and lemon juice and a few slices of bread. Serve hot. Serves 6.

MAKROUDH (Date-Filled Pastry)

> 1 lb. dates ("alig")
> 1¾ cups olive oil
> ¼ cup salted butter
> ½ tsp. cinnamon
> 2¾ lbs. coarse semolina (hard wheat)
> 1 tbls. salt
> ½ lb. "castor" sugar (granulated)
> juice of 1 small lemon (3 tbls.)

Wash and dry dates carefully, and remove stones. Reduce to a smooth paste with 1/3 cup oil and cinnamon. Heat the remainder of the oil with butter slightly. Measure semolina into a fairly large bowl and pour oil over it, adding salt. Using a little warm water, mix the whole to a fairly stiff consistency.

Roll the paste to 1/2 inch thick on an oiled board, and cut into strips 3 inches wide. Place a ribbon of the date paste, 1/2 inch thick, down the middle of each strip, and fold over, bringing the edges together. A flat, engraved wooden mold, is usually used to press a pattern on to the surface of the *makroudh* dough. Press this mold firmly into the strips of the date-filled dough to flatten them to the thickness of 1/2 inch, and trim off the edges with a knife.

Bake in hot oven (400 degrees) for 25-30 minutes. Make a syrup from sugar, lemon juice and water and dip pastry in syrup. Drain on paper towel.

SHAKSHOUKA (Sausages with Tomatoes and Green Peppers)

On a spring or summer day when you simply cannot think of what to fix for lunch, reach for the recipe for *Shakshouka*, surprisingly simple and delicious. Even the most inexperienced cook can throw the ingredients together. If your family is very hungry, throw in a few hard-boiled eggs at the end of cooking.

2 medium onions, sliced
1/3 cup olive oil
a few sausages (mergaz)
5 medium tomatoes, chopped
½ tbls. harissa
½ tbls. paprika
½ lb hot peppers

Slice and brown onions in oil. Add a few pieces of sausage. Chop tomatoes, remove seeds and add to onions with harissa, paprika, and a pinch of salt. Cover with water and simmer. As soon as the sausage is cooked, remove seeds of peppers, cut them up roughly, add and cook further for 15 minutes. Check for seasoning and serve hot. Serves 6.

SLATA MESHWIYA (Barbecued Salad)

3 tomatoes, medium
½ lb. sweet green peppers
2-3 hot peppers
1 small onion
1 small pickled lemon, sliced
1 tbls. capers
juice of 1 small lemon (fresh)
1/3 cup olive oil
3½ oz. canned tuna fish
2 hard-boiled eggs

Grill tomatoes, green peppers, hot peppers and onion over hot coals. Peel and remove seeds from peppers and tomatoes; peel onion. Cut all vegetables into small pieces, add sliced lemon and capers. Mix well, adding lemon juice and salt to taste. Sprinkle with olive oil. Garnish with tuna fish and sliced hard-boiled eggs. Serves 3.

TAJEEN (Meat Pies)

Tajeen is homemade patties served to add variety to the menu. They are simply meat or chicken mixed with eggs and a cheese flavoring. This dish is called *Tajeen* after the king of the Tunisians who used to cook it.

1 onion, chopped
1½ lbs. lamb or beef, cut into 1 inch cubes
1 tbls. olive oil
1 tbls. butter
1 tbls. tomato sauce
¼ cup water
½ cup small green peas
¼ cup grated Parmesan cheese
6 eggs

Chop onions finely and mix with meat. Heat oil in a 6-quart saucepan until smoking. Add meat, onions, butter, tomato sauce; salt and pepper to taste. Stir well. When meat is well-browned, pour water in, just enough to barely cover the meat. When water boils, let it simmer on low heat and cover for 15 minutes. Uncover, add peas, and mix well. Sprinkle in grated cheese. Remove from heat, mix eggs into the preparation. (Do not beat eggs beforehand.) Put the mixture in a hot greased 10" x 20" pan and bake in a 350 degree oven for 1/2 hour. The *Tajeen* can be eaten hot or cold and leftovers can be frozen. It is delicious cold, cut into bite-sized pieces and served with rose or red wine. Serves 6.

TUNISIAN BRIK WITH EGG

This delicate filled pastry is delicious but difficult to eat. Care must be taken in eating a *brik* or it will be messy. Hold the *brik* in both hands with the longest side at a vertical angle and start eating from the top, ending by sucking out the egg.

1 recipe for pie pastry
1, 7 oz. can tuna fish
6 tsp. capers
8 oz. white cheese, grated
parsley, chopped
6 eggs
cooking fat

Roll out pastry to make six 8 inch squares. In center of each square place a portion of tuna fish, capers, white cheese, and parsley, making a nest into which the raw egg is dropped. Fold over pastry to form a triangle and seal edges. Place in deep boiling fat and cook for about 5 minutes or until pastry has turned light brown and is crisp. Drain on paper toweling. Serves 6.

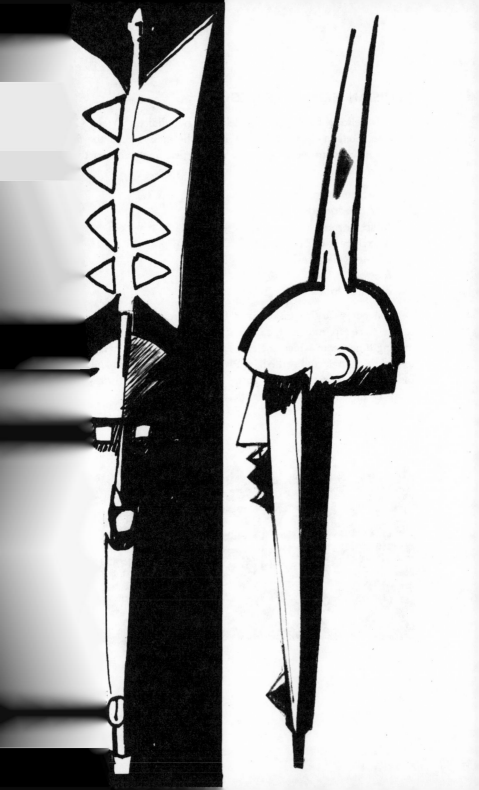

UPPER VOLTA (BURKINA FASO)

The primary exports here are livestock and an edible fat called karite. The natives grow beans and millet for subsistence, and take great pride in cultivating la mangue greffe, a hybrid mango which has no trace of the turpentine taste of the parent fruit. We have included two popular mango dishes here, and you may also use the mango for compotes, salads, and desserts.

Suggested Menu Plan:

Breakfast: Mango Omelette and Coffee or Tea

Lunch or Dinner: Mango Chutney, Meat Curry, Bread

BURKINA FASO **Helmet Mask, Bobo Fing Tribe.**

MANGO CHUTNEY

6 large mangoes, not too ripe
1 cup cider vinegar
3 ½ cups brown sugar
3 cups raisins
1 cup water
1 lemon, ground whole
1 orange, ground whole
2 cloves garlic, mashed
¼ tsp. ground cloves
1 ½ tsp. dry ginger or 1 inch ginger root, chopped
¼ tsp. red pepper
¼ tsp. black pepper
1 ½ tsp. salt
juice of 5 limes
juice of 1 lemon

Cook mangoes, vinegar, sugar and raisins until tender. Add all the rest of the ingredients except the lime and lemon juices. Simmer for 1 hour or more until well blended. Add juices. Taste. You make *chutney* to your own taste, so you may add onions, sour apples, or any other condiment which strikes your fancy. Taste for the vinegar especially; you may want to add more, depending on the kind you use. Makes 3 pints.

MANGO OMELETTE

2 mangoes
3 tbls. sugar
juice of 1 small lemon (3 tbls.)
4 eggs
¼ cup flour
½ cup milk
2 tbls. butter

Skin and cut mangoes into small pieces. Place them in a sauce-pan and mix with sugar and lemon juice. Heat for 5 minutes. Beat egg yolks, and slowly add to them flour, milk and beaten egg whites. Add this liquid to mangoes. Melt butter in a frying pan and fry half the mango mixture at a time. Serve sprinkled with sugar. Serves 2.

ZAMBIA

The staple food is mealie meal, and the people of Zambia consume 2.5 million bags of it a year. Mealie meal is prepared in endless ways, from the simple mealie meal porridge to sweet beer brewed from mealie meal fermented with roots. The favorite main dish is chicken and vegetables (beans, cassava, or sweet potatoes).

Suggested Menu Plan:

Breakfast: Mealie Meal Porridge and Coffee

Lunch: Baked Tomatoes and Green Mealies, Rice

Dinner: Fish Stew, Green Mealie Bread, Mealie Meal Pudding

BAKED TOMATOES AND GREEN MEALIES

    3 cups (5 cobs) green mealies (raw corn)
    1 small onion, chopped
    2 tomatoes, chopped
    2 eggs, separated
    ¼ cup oil or shortening
    2 tbls. breadcrumbs

ZAMBIA: Wiko youth on display.

Boil mealies on the cob until tender. Cut mealies off from the cob and mix with finely chopped onions, tomatoes, and beaten egg yolks. Add salt and pepper to taste. Beat the egg whites stiffly; fold into the mixture. Sprinkle breadcrumbs on the top and dab with oil. Bake in a moderate oven (325 degrees) until set. Serve with mealie-meal porridge or bread. Serves 5.

CABBAGE STEW

    1 lb. cabbage
    2 medium onions, chopped
    1-3 tomatoes, chopped
    2 tbls, oil or shortening
    curry powder
    1 cup water

Wash and cut up vegetables. Fry onion in hot oil until light brown. Add curry powder, salt and pepper to taste. Add water and cabbage; steam until soft (about 20 minutes). Add chopped tomatoes and cook for 10 more minutes. Stir all together and serve with meat. For a larger quantity of stew, add the gravy from the meat. Also, potatoes may be substituted for half the quantity of cabbage if prefered. Serves 3-4.

CHICKEN SOUP

    12 cups water
    ½ lb. chicken
    2 small carrots, diced
    2 small potatoes, diced
    2 small onions, chopped

Cook diced meat in water until tender, about 1 hour. Add diced carrots and potatoes, chopped onions, and simmer for 15 minutes. Salt and pepper to taste. Serve. May be thickened if desired by mixing a smooth paste of water and 1/2 cup flour and stirring into soup. For special occasions, any cereal, like mealie meal or wheat, may be added to the soup. Serves 4.

FISH STEW

2 large onions, chopped
2 tbls. oil or shortening
2 large carrots, chopped
2 large potatoes, chopped
2 large parsnips, chopped
1 lb. fish filets
2 cups water
¼ cup flour

Chop and fry onion in hot oil until light brown. Peel and chop the other vegetables and add to fried onion. Season with salt and pepper to taste, and cut the fish into neat pieces. Add fish to vegetables. Steam over gentle heat for about 30 minutes. Make a sauce from the oil, flour, and water. Add to stew and cook gently for 5 minutes or more. Serves 4.

GREEN MEALIE BREAD

2 cups ground green mealies (raw corn)
2 cups flour
2 tbls. sugar
1 tsp salt
4 tsp. baking powder
cold milk or water

Mix dry ingredients together. Add enough milk or water to form a stiff dough. Put the mixture in a greased loaf pan and steam for about 1 1/2 hours. Serve hot with meat stew, or serve cold with sweet or sour milk. Makes one 1-lb. loaf.

Note: 1 tsp. yeast may be used instead of baking powder. But then the dough must be left to rise. If yeast is used, all ingredients must be warm.

MEALIE MEAL PORRIDGE

4 cups milk
1 cup mealie meal (corn meal)

Boil milk. Add mealie meal and a little cold milk, mixing to a soft paste. Boil slowly for about 15 minutes, stirring to avoid lumps. Serve sprinkled with sugar. Serves 4.

MEALIE MEAL PUDDING

1 cup mealie meal (corn meal)
2 cups milk
2 tsp. sugar
1 egg
pinch of salt

Boil milk, sugar and salt. Make a soft paste of the mealie meal and boiled milk or water as is needed. Simmer until cooked. Separate the egg; whisk the white. Stir in the yolk. Fold in the white. Spoon into individual dishes. Serves 4.

MEALIE MEAL RISSOLES

1 medium onion, chopped
2 eggs
1 cup flour
4 cups water or milk
1 ½ cups mealie meal (corn meal)
½ cup oil or shortening

Peel, chop and fry onion until light brown. Beat eggs; add to onions with flour. Add water or milk. Salt and pepper to taste. To prepare the mealie meal or corn meal, add as much boiling water to it as is necessary to make a smooth paste. Stir and cook for 10 minutes; remove from heat to cool. When cool, mince finely and add to rissole mixture. Shape into small balls and fry in very hot oil. Serves 6.

INDEX

NOTES